THE ONE WHO LED AN ARMY

D1615711

THREE FRENCH SAINTS
THE ONE WHO LED AN ARMY

Joan of Arc
(1412-1431)

Críostóir Ó Floinn

the columba press

First published in 2009 by
the columba press
55A Spruce Avenue, Stillorgan Industrial Park,
Blackrock, Co Dublin

Cover by Bill Bolger
Origination by The Columba Press
Printed by Athenaeum Press, Gateshead

ISBN 978-1-85607-658-6

Table of Contents

CHAPTER ONE

Setting the Scene

In order to understand the story of any historical character, it is necessary to have a sufficient knowledge of the period and the society in which that person lived. Even what has been rightly called 'the greatest story ever told' contains incidents the significance of which will be lost unless the reader is aware of the social, religious and political situation in Palestine at the time: why, for instance, when the Jewish High Priest declared, in what was an unwittingly ambiguous and portentous utterance, that it was 'necessary that one man should die for the people', it was the Roman governor who, albeit against his own conscience, finally condemned Jesus to death? Biographies of Julius Caesar, Napoleon Bonaparte, and Adolf Hitler, whatever interest they might have in common as regards the horrors of war, will be fully meaningful only in the historical context in which their respective contributions to those horrors were accomplished. The public career of the young French girl, Jeanne d'Arc, on the stage of European politics was brief – one year as a warrior, one year as a prisoner – but the results of that career, in her own time and subsequently, have made her one of the most interesting figures in the history of France and of the entire world. Her life and death have also resulted in her being made both Patron of France and a saint of the Catholic Church. To understand why, a chronological narration of the events of her life would not suffice; it is essential to consider the context of that life.

In the year 1412, when Jeanne d'Arc was born in the little village of Domrémy, in the province of Lorraine near the border with Germany, France and Europe were very different from what they are now. Let us take Europe first: the two most important facts are that America had not yet been discovered – it would be in 1492 – and that Europe was still Catholic, apart from some parts of Spain where the expulsion of the Moors was not yet complete – it would be in 1492 with the surrender of Granada to the armies of the Catholic sovereigns, Ferdinand and Isabella. Europe would remain Catholic for another hundred years, until the Augustinian monk, Martin Luther, publicly declared in 1517 his plan to reform the church, ending up by leaving it and establishing his own version of Christianity.

While England had been a single kingdom since its conquest in 1066 by William, Duke of Normandy, some other countries were very different from their present status. Much of what is now Belgium, an independent state only since 1830, and some areas in the Rhineland, were part of the realm of the French Duke of Burgundy, while Italy and Germany did not become the unified countries we know today until 1870. In 1412 they were still divided into independent provinces or kingdoms linked only by language and commerce. One of those local rulers was the Pope, who controlled the papal states around Rome and was often involved in the military and political affairs of Italy and Europe. In his proper role, as Vicar of Christ and Head of the Catholic Church, the Pope was nominally the spiritual head of Europe with the power to excommunicate or even depose rulers. He also had to deal with heretics and dissident would-be reformers as well as with those princes and kings who made use of them for their own purposes, as the German princes made use of Luther in the next century, and Henry VIII of England, initially honoured by the Pope for his opposition to Luther, later used some native recalcitrant clerics to make himself head of the church in England.

Another recurrent problem for the Pope was the dispute about whether the Pope or the general council of the bishops of the church should be the final arbiter in matters of doctrine. Strange as it may seem in our time, when universities have deteriorated into mere dispensers of qualifications in the various branches of arts, science and technology, the principal subjects of study in the medieval university were theology and philosophy – many universities had developed from schools attached to monasteries or cathedrals – and the Pope's most active opponents in those doctrinal disputes were some of the theologians of the universities (a further complication in all such disputes was the partisan academic opposition between the theologians of the religious orders, especially the Dominicans and the Franciscans). As with the heretics and reformers – many of whom were products of the universities – these anti-Papal theologians were opportune instruments in the ambitions of kings and princes. The University of Paris, in particular, became notorious in this regard, and the fate of Jeanne d'Arc was influenced by the involvement of its learned doctors in the political scene. Because Latin was the language of all official documents such as treaties and political marriage alliances, scholarly churchmen were often employed as emissaries and negotiators, furthering their own ambitions in the process.

Three great crises, social, religious and political, respectively, were affecting Europe generally when Jeanne d'Arc was born. The memory of the Black Death or Great Plague was still vivid, and its effects were still felt in economic and social matters. Only half a century before her birth, the bubonic plague had swept across from Asia and cut the population of Europe by almost half (it was to recur in the coming centuries). In the religious life of Europe, the Great Schism had been a scandal for forty years, from 1378 to 1417, with two, and at one time three, different claimants to the office of Pope. This had all arisen from a papal election which was considered by the cardinals taking part to have been influenced by threats and violence, and therefore invalid. It became more complicated when a French Pope took refuge in Avignon and the nations of Europe took sides in the dispute accordingly. The third crisis, the political one, was that in which the career and death of Jeanne d'Arc played a direct part. This was the final stage of the so-called Hundred Years War, a series of intermittent wars between England and France, lasting from 1337 to 1443 (Jeanne's two-year career spanned 1429-1431). In *A Popular History of the Catholic Church*, the renowned English scholar, Fr Philip Hughes, sums up the conflict in a passage that is worth quoting in full because of its reference to the subject of this present work:

> England was engaged on one of the greater wickednesses of its long history in that succession of pillaging raids on France that goes by the name of the Hundred Years War, and the losses to Catholicism that ensued from this Catholic power's plundering of a neighbouring Catholic country were such that, in the end, Providence intervened directly and, to rid the country of the scourge, sent the inspired generalship of the Lorraine peasant girl, St Joan of Arc (1429).

In order to understand the significance of the political dispute between England and France in the life and death of Jeanne d'Arc, it is necessary to go back as far as William the Conqueror, as he is called, the ruler of the province of Normandy in France who invaded England in 1066. Having had himself crowned King of England on Christmas Day 1066, and having ruthlessly suppressed the Anglo-Saxons whose ancestors had invaded England from Germany five centuries before him, William continued to regard himself as French rather than English – French became the language of the ruling class in England for nearly three hundred years – and he maintained his links with his domains in France and his ambition to extend them further. He was actually besieging the town of Mantes near Paris in 1087 when he fell from his horse and suffered a fatal injury from which he died at the Convent of St Gervais near Rouen. He was buried at Caen in his native Normandy.

William's successors on the throne of England continued to regard the English Channel as a mere sea-link between what could become an Anglo-French dual kingdom. When Henry V routed the French at the Battle of Agincourt in 1415, he was in a position to dictate the terms of the Treaty of Troyes (1420) which awarded him Catherine, daughter of King Charles VI of France, as his bride and promised that their son would become king of both countries. This effectively disinherited the rightful heir to the throne of France, Charles, younger brother of Catherine. He was the Dauphin to whom the young peasant girl, Jeanne, came to tell him that she had been sent by God to lead his army and restore him to his inheritance as King of France.

It may come as a surprise to some readers to learn that at this period Scotland, still an independent kingdom, was an ally of France, with Scottish troops and commanders taking part in the fighting at Orléans and other places – one of the commanders is referred to in French records as Hugh Kenede. The King of Scotland during the lifetime of Jeanne was James I (1406-1437), not to be confused with James I of England who was also James VI of Scotland and who became the first king of the united king-doms on the death of Elizabeth I in 1603 (Elizabeth had sent his mother, her own cousin, Mary Queen of Scots, to the scaffold in 1587 after holding her prisoner in England for 19 years). As a boy of twelve, James I of Scotland was sent away by his father, Robert III, to avoid the fate of his older brother, assassinated by the king's enemies in a civil war; but on his way to France he was captured by the English and held prisoner for ransom. He spent 18 years in England, where he was well educated at the court, and was allowed back to Scotland on the death of his father in 1406, the Scottish Parliament having agreed by treaty that the ransom would be paid over a period of six years.

As has been seen in the case of William, Duke of Normandy and subsequently King of England, there were also powerful local rulers in France who, although nominally subject to the king, were in effect independent lords in their own domains. One of these was the Duke of Burgundy whose territory extended into Flanders and the Rhineland. Because of a feud with the Duke of Orléans, the Duke of Burgundy had allied himself with the English power in France. In the year when Jeanne was born, the northern part of France, almost one-third of the country, was in the hands of the English, as well as the area of Guyenne on the south-west coast near Spain.

A further political complication was the number of fortified cities. Some of these were isolated in hostile territory, maintaining their hazardous allegiance, French or English or Burgundian, in an area not controlled by the power to which they were loyal. Although it was at this period that artillery was being developed into a truly destructive weapon, the small cannon were not yet capable of demolishing the thick walls of such cities; mounted on the walls, they were actually as useful in defence as in attack; although often as much of a hazard to the gunners as to the enemy. Fortified cities could hold out for a long period, hoping for the arrival of a relief force, if they had sufficient supplies of food and water. A direct attack on such a fortified city involved scaling ladders and bloody hand-to-hand fighting. In open warfare, the armour-clad knights on horseback were the equivalent of the modern tank, while a flight of arrows prefigured the machine-gun – one such arrow killed the Anglo-Saxon, Harold, at Hastings in 1066, and the English longbow won the Battle of Agincourt for Henry V. A knight taken prisoner was held for ransom – the Duke of Orléans, captured at Agincourt at the age of twenty-four, spent the next twenty-five years as a noble prisoner in England, from where he continued to conduct the affairs of his duchy through his half-brother and officials, until the enormous ransom of 120,000 écus of gold finally secured his liberation. The common soldiers in a routed army, being of no value, were not taken prisoner; their only safety lay in what might be termed the Horation run – the Roman poet, Horace, whose immortal line, *Dulce et decorum est pro patria mori*, embellishes many a war memorial, admits candidly in another of his odes that he and his friend threw away their shields and swords and fled from the rout at Philippi, BC 42.

Because there were not yet formal armies, the troops engaged in wars had to be supplied by the king himself and his barons from their own feudal subjects. These were supplemented by mercenaries, commanded by their own leader, who were ready to fight on any side that would pay them. They were a cause of terror to the civilian population in any country; in the intervals of peace, they often behaved like ruthless bandits, using looting and extortion to support and enrich themselves.

Finally, the modern reader must adjust mentally to an era when ships were still wooden and powered by the wind, when the telephone and the radio, the steam engine, the car and television, did not exist, and only birds flew in the air; in short, transport depended on the horse-drawn wagon, and communication on the human messenger, on foot or on horseback; if horse or rider came to grief in any way, the message did not arrive. News travelled slowly – it could have taken months or even years for the common people all over Europe to learn about such things as the dispute about the rival Popes. Unless they saw the smoke rising from burning houses or crops in the distance, the inhabitants of any town or village might not know that marauding soldiers or bandits were in their area until they were attacked. Printed books and newspapers were unknown – Gutenberg invented his printing press around 1450, twenty years after the death of Jeanne d'Arc – and most people, like Jeanne herself, were illiterate. Although Europe was officially Catholic, people everywhere believed in magic and witches, and remnants of pagan customs were still part of local life. Heresy was considered not only a heinous offence against God by the church, but the equivalent of treason to the state; if found guilty of heresy by a church tribunal, the heretic was handed over to the state authorities for sentence and execution. Torture was commonly used to extract confessions or evidence, many crimes were capital offences, and methods of execution were gruesome. What with wars and disease, recurrent famines and other causes, life expectancy was short in comparison with our own day.

Now that the scene has been set, we can say, in dramatic terms: Enter Jeanne, a young peasant girl, aged about sixteen.

CHAPTER TWO

Who was she?

There are few personages in history who have been investigated so thoroughly, during her lifetime and ever since her death, both by friends and enemies, by believers and cynics, as the girl who is now known in her own country as Jeanne d'Arc and in English as Joan of Arc. It is something of an anomaly, then, that she never used that title herself. When she was formally asked at her trial in 1431 to state her name and surname, her reply was recorded thus: *'Dans mon pays on m'appelait Jeannette, mais on m'appela Jeanne quand je vins en France'* ('In my country I was called Jeannette, but when I came into France I was called Jeanne') – by France she meant that part of the country under the control of the Dauphin, heir to the throne, rather than the areas controlled by his enemies, the Burgundians and the English. Of the many letters she dictated and signed – like all peasants of her time, she was illiterate – three survive, and they are signed Jehanne.

With regard to her surname, French scholars are generally agreed that the original form was Darc, the form d'Arc coming into use later in imitation of surnames in which the apostrophe indicated either family or place of origin. Surnames were not generally used in those times – Jeanne told her judges that girls in her country were often known by their mother's name added to their own; her own mother was known as Isabelle Romée, a surname commonly given to people because they had made a pilgrimage. From her first appearance on the public scene until her death, the only title Jeanne used as an addition to her personal name was *la Pucelle*. This is rendered in English as the Maid – she is often referred to as The Maid of Orléans – which, although not now likely to be given the Victorian social meaning of a domestic servant, might be taken as meaning simply a young unmarried woman. In the original French, however, and in its consistent use by Jeanne, the connotation is more moral than social, reminding us of the older English usage linking the words maid and maidenhead. A modern French dictionary defines the noun *pucelle* as 'chaste person, virgin, maid'. The public use of that appellation constituted a statement by Jeanne that she was a virgin whose life was consecrated to God for the purpose of fulfilling the mission for which she claimed to have been chosen. That its significance was so regarded by friends and enemies alike will be seen from the importance attached to it in the investigations and interrogations to which she and her claim were subjected.

The many official inquiries into Jeanne and her background have left us with the information that her parents were highly regarded as good Catholics and honest members of their community. They owned their house and about fifty acres of land; they also rented some land from the priest. Her father, Jacques Darc, was an important civic personage in their village of Domrémy, and her mother's brother became parish priest in a neighbouring village. All the reports, and they were many and professional, about Jeanne herself came up with nothing that could blemish her character in the slightest. She was by all accounts a lively and healthy girl, a dutiful daughter, helping her mother with household work and her father in the fields, and she was considered by all her friends and neighbours to be sincerely devout and very diligent in the observance of her religious duties – one man who had been her contemporary as a teenager recalled that he used to tease her with being so pious. She declared at her trial that she was only thirteen years old when she first heard a heavenly voice speaking to her in her father's garden. At her trial it was brought against her that she had once been charged before an ecclesiastical court in her own area with breaking a promise of marriage, but she vigorously rebutted the charge, declaring that she had never made such a promise to anybody, and was duly acquitted .

Jeanne had a sister and three brothers; it was one of the latter who later provided the strange information that their father once dreamt that his daughter, Jeanne, had gone away with soldiers, and on awakening told her brothers that he would prefer to see her drowned. The fact that Jeanne eventually went away from home to engage in military campaigns might cause some people to interpret that paternal nightmare as of special prophetic significance; but Jacques Darc was not the only father who would have feared such a fate for his daughter, in that century or in many others before or since. One has only to consider the origin of the colloquial phrase, 'to be sent to Coventry', as given in Brewster's *Dictionary of Phrase and Fable:* 'It is said that the citizens of Coventry had such a dislike of soldiers that a woman seen speaking to one was instantly tabooed; hence when a soldier was sent to Coventry he was cut off from all social intercourse.' And in *Pride and Prejudice* Jane Austen makes dramatic use of the effect of a rascal in uniform on a scatty young girl and the social consequences for the entire family. When Jeanne Darc left home at her first attempt to pursue her mission, she was accompanied by a close relative as her protector and her father seems to have made no objection to her departure. One of her brothers joined her later and was with her all through her military campaigns.

Now that we know something of Jeanne la Pucelle and her people, it would be as well to learn something about the other chief protagonist in the drama of her life and death, Charles, the Dauphin of France. From her first appearance on the public stage, Jeanne proclaimed that her purpose was, by the aid of the King of Heaven, firstly to relieve the siege being laid to the strategic city of Orléans by the English, and then to bring the Dauphin to Reims to be crowned King of France – Reims being the traditional site of that ceremony, as Scone was for the Kings of Scotland. Apart from historians and francophiles, other people may not be *au fait* with the term Dauphin or understand its significance in the context of Jeanne's mission. The Dauphin of France was the equivalent of the Crown Prince in other countries, the heir to the throne. The Dauphin to whom the peasant girl, Jeanne la Pucelle, came with her extraordinary message in March 1429, was eventually to become King Charles VII. He would not have been heir to the throne at all but for the death of other children in the royal family. He was the eleventh of twelve children born to King Charles VI and his queen, Isabeau of Bavaria. He was the fourth of the five sons, and came to the title of Dauphin only because the three sons born before him died, the first as an infant, the next as a young boy, the third as a youth of eighteen.

When Jeanne met up with him, the Dauphin Charles was twenty-six years old and he was in a desperate situation, trying to make good his claim to the throne against the combined might of England and Burgundy. As has been seen, he had been disinherited by the Treaty of Troyes which guaranteed the two kingdoms of France and England to the infant King Henry VI of England. Paris and the northern part of France were in the hands of the English, and they were now laying siege to Orléans, the taking of which strategic city would open the way for the conquest of the rest of France. If he had been able to rely on solid military support from any source, Charles would probably have given short shrift to the peasant girl who arrived at his court with a promise that she would bring him help from heaven – and also with the threat that if he did not accept that help, he would get no other.

Descriptions of Charles are not flattering. He was not physically impressive, being thin and not very robust; also, he had an unbalanced gait and knees that were best kept hidden by long robes which gave him a more majestic air. Portraits show him as rather sad and gloomy, but he was a cultivated man, fluent in Latin, interested in history and science, and able to play the harp. He was also solitary and distrustful, sometimes promoting people to a certain level and then taking pleasure in humbling them. Although he was the first King of France to acknowledge a mistress by a title, and his final years were devoted to pleasure rather than to affairs of state, he has been judged by historians to have left France, after thirty-seven years on the throne, in much better condition at his death in 1461 than the sorry state it was in at the beginning of the century when a chronicler described it as 'turned upside down, a footstool for mankind, the winepress of the English, a bootwipe for brigands'.

CHAPTER THREE

The Girl who heard Voices

When King Henry V of England, the victor of Agincourt, died in August 1422, his only son and heir, Henry VI, was just nine months old. This was the child who, according to the Treaty of Troyes signed in 1420, was supposed to unite France and England under one crown. On his death-bed, Henry V entrusted his brother, John, Duke of Bedford, with the duty of achieving that inheritance in spite of the opposition of the French. Bedford was also one of the regents ruling England until the heir came of age, other regents being the child's French mother, Catherine, sister of the Dauphin, and his great-uncle, Henry Beaufort, Cardinal Archbishop of Winchester. Bedford left affairs in England to the regency council while he vigorously pursued the military campaign in France in alliance with Duke Philip of Burgundy whose sister, Anne, was his wife. When the cautious Duke of Burgundy refused Bedford's offer of the regency of France on behalf of Henry VI, Bedford took on that office also as a further step towards securing the two kingdoms for his nephew.

While his military victories in the field increased the English hold on the northern part of France and made the cause of the Dauphin more hopeless, Bedford realised that the existence in Anglo-Burgundian territory of fortified cities loyal to the Dauphin could not be tolerated. The city of Vaucouleurs, situated on the River Meuse in the North-East of France, was one of those fortified cities. Its lord and military commander, Robert de Baudricourt, steadfastly maintained his allegiance to Charles and to the French cause, but the city itself was in that sector of France controlled by the English, with the lands of their ally, the Duke of Burgundy, to the south and east. In May 1428, the garrison and the people of Vaucouleurs were aware that their city was likely to see a hostile army approaching at any time. Robert de Baudricourt had made preparations for a long siege and he would have been expecting daily to receive news from his scouts and spies of the approach of an Anglo-Burgundian force. The news he heard one day in the middle of May, was very different. His squire, Robert de Metz, told him that a young peasant girl dressed in red had arrived in the city from some village on the eastern border. She was accompanied by a man she called her uncle – he turned out to be the husband of a cousin – and she was going about asking people in the streets and soldiers on the battlements to bring her to speak with the Lord Robert because, she said, she had news for him from her Lord in heaven that concerned the Dauphin and France. The people, and the soldiers especially, were making fun of this girl, dressed in a red overall garment, and her humble peasant protector.

When Robert de Baudricourt, whether out of curiosity or annoyance, finally allowed this strange pair into his presence, the girl told him that her name was Jeanne, that she was about seventeen years old, and that she had walked, with her protector, from her native village, Domrémy, because voices from heaven had instructed her to come to him. He was to tell the Dauphin to hold out, but not to engage in open conflict with his English and Burgundian enemies because help would come to him from heaven before the middle of Lent next year. The kingdom of France belonged to God, she said, and the Dauphin would regain it, in spite of his enemies, and hold it as a fief from God. She herself would lead the Dauphin to be anointed king.

The seasoned warrior who was Lord defender of the fortified city of Vaucouleurs reacted bluntly to this astounding declaration. He ordered the embarrassed peasant, Durand Laxart, to take that silly girl home and give her a few slaps to put manners on her. That done, he got back to the business in hand, the defence of his city against the impending siege.

He did not have long to wait. Just a month later, in June 1428, the people of the surrounding villages were crowding into the city as scouts reported the approach of a Burgundian force. The siege of Vaucouleurs did not last long. Although other such cities had surrendered, it became obvious to the besiegers that this city was so well fortified and supplied, and its governor so determined to defend it, that troops would have to be deployed around it for a long time in order to reduce it by starvation; with the danger that they might themselves be attacked by a relieving force combining with the garrison. A month after they arrived, the besiegers were packing their tents and moving away. A compromise had been reached – the siege would be abandoned, leaving the city of Vaucouleurs still in French control, on condition that Robert de Baudricourt promised that he would not engage in direct military action against the Burgundians in the surrounding area.

In that same month, July 1428, the people in Domrémy and the neighbouring villages were alarmed by reports of Burgundian forces moving towards the east. With her parents, her sister and three brothers, Jeanne was a refugee. Driving their cattle before them, the peasants headed for their local fortified city, Neuf-château, where they stayed until the hostile army had passed on – they could judge that passage by the smoke from their burning crops.

A few months later, in October 1428, the Duke of Bedford turned his attention to the main project of his current campaign. He laid siege to the city of Orléans, situated in a central position on the dividing line between the English and French territories. It was also central politically as controlling the route south to Bourges where the Dauphin had established his court while nervously awaiting the outcome of the war that could gain him the throne or cost him his head.

When news of the siege of Orléans reached him, Robert de Baudricourt, the knight-commander of Vaucouleurs, knew the implications for himself and for the French cause if that city fell into the hands of the English. He spent the winter preparing for a possible assault on his own city as soon as the spring allowed hostilities to begin again. When they did, the news coming from the Orléans area was increasingly bad; the English were so intent on taking that pivotally strategic city that they had begun methodically to cut off the exits with the erection of temporary wooden forts, known as *bastides*. These were connected with earthworks, and could be big enough to house troops. If the encirclement of Orléans by such structures could be completed, it would be impossible to bring supplies into the beleaguered garrison.

On 13 February, the first Sunday in Lent 1429, Robert de Baudricourt might well have been engaged in his command post like Caesar in the poem by Yeats: 'Our master, Caesar, is in the tent / Where maps are spread / His eyes fixed upon nothing / His hand under his head / Like a long-leggèd fly upon the stream / His mind moves upon silence', when his strategic reverie was disturbed by his squire coming to inform him that the peasant girl from Domrémy, whom he had thrown out last May, was back in town again with her protective relation, Durand Laxart. She claimed to have further instructions from her heavenly voices for the defender of Vaucouleurs. Worse still, the townspeople, and even some of the soldiers, were not laughing at her now; some were even beginning to believe that she was a holy girl who really had some kind of a message from God, and they were offering her hospitality and help.

Instead of clapping them both in chains, which may have been his first impulse, Robert de Baudricourt decided to hear this latest bit of news from heaven. It was even more audacious than the first message: now, Jeanne told him, she had to go to meet the Dauphin, Charles, before mid-Lent because she was appointed to bring him help from heaven that would raise the siege of Orléans and have him crowned King of France at Reims. If the Dauphin did not get this heavenly help through Jeanne, he would get no other, and Robert de Baudricourt himself was to supply her with a horse and an escort to take her to the Dauphin who was then residing at Chinon, a distance of eleven days' ride from Vaucouleurs. He threw her out again, presumably with more threatening instructions to her guardian. This time, however, Jeanne did not return to Domrémy. The commander's squire and servants would have kept him informed about her, that she was lodging with some people in the town who were among those who believed in her mission, and impressing more of the citizens and soldiers with her sincerity and conviction. Then he heard that, having been provided with a horse by her guardian and a supporting citizen, Jeanne had set out with them on the long and dangerous road through enemy Burgundian territory, heading for Chinon. She did not go far. She told her companions that she had done wrong in not keeping to the instructions given her by her voices; she must convince Robert de Baudricourt to play his part by providing her with a proper escort. She turned back and was welcomed even more warmly by the people of the city.

While she waited for another opportunity to appeal to the commander, Jeanne gave the first public evidence, outside her own family and neighbours, of the personal piety and holiness that was to impress everyone she met henceforth, whether friends or enemies. A young priest at the local church of Notre Dame testified later that he used to see her at Mass every morning, staying on for a long time afterwards to kneel in prayer before the statue of Our Lady.

By this time, news of the strange young woman and her claim of celestial instructions had spread beyond the city of Vaucouleurs. One day, a messenger came to the city from the neighbouring duchy of Lorraine. The Duke of Lorraine, a vassal of the Duke of Burgundy, invited the girl from Domrémy to come and visit him at his castle in the city of Nancy; as her journey would involve passing through Burgundian territory, he sent her a guarantee of safe conduct. Duke Charles of Lorraine had been a notorious participant in the Anglo-French wars, and he was also a noted profligate, rejecting his wife and siring sons with a local girl; but now he was old and unwell, and he probably hoped, if this girl he had heard about were really inspired by heaven, that she might be able to do something for him by her prayers. That was the subject he discussed with Jeanne, only to be told, with the directness that was to be characteristic of her conversations with people in all classes of society, that she knew nothing about such matters; however, she promised to pray to God for his recovery if he would give her his son and some men-at-arms for the cause of France (the 'son' she mentioned was really the Duke's son-in-law, René of Anjou, who was also the brother-in-law of the Dauphin – again we see the lax use of such familial terminology).

The Duke was also reproached by Jeanne because of his immoral life; he seems to have taken this reproof without rancour and to have been impressed by Joan. He made her a present of a fine horse and gave some money to her faithful guardian, Durand Laxart, to cover the expenses of their journey. Others, including Robert de Metz, the squire of Robert de Baudricourt of Vaucouleurs, are thought to have accompanied Jeanne on that journey. They would have seen further evidence of this young girl's piety – Jeanne took the opportunity of her safe conduct to visit shrines in the area that would otherwise have been inaccessible.

On her return to Vaucouleurs, Jeanne found its commander in an altered mood. He had taken note of the increasing support of the citizens for her proclaimed mission. He must also have been swayed by the interest shown in her by the Duke of Lorraine. His own thirty-year-old noble squire, Robert de Metz, was already a strong supporter of the girl from Domrémy, although initially, as he admitted afterwards, he had treated her flippantly. 'When I first met her,' he testified, 'I asked her jokingly: My dear, what are you doing here? Wouldn't it be better to get rid of the king and for all of us to become English?' Jeanne replied, as always without losing her composure: 'I have come to the king's territory to speak with Robert de Baudricourt, so that he would bring me, or have me brought by others, to the king himself; but he pays no attention to me, or to what I say; nevertheless, before the middle of Lent it is necessary that I get to the king, even if it means I have to wear my legs away to the knees; because there is no one else, not a king nor a duke, nor even the daughter of the King of Scotland, who can recover the kingdom of France, nor will he have any help unless from me, although I would much prefer to be at home spinning wool with my poor mother, because this is not my state, but I must go and I must do it, since my Lord wishes me so to do.'

Taken aback by such a reply to his raillery, he asked her in more serious vein: 'But who is your Lord.' Jeanne replied: 'God.' The gallant young squire was won over completely. He says: 'Then, I promised the Maid, placing my hand in hers as a sign of good faith, that I, with God's help, would guide her to the king. I asked her when did she wish to leave, and she said: Better now than tomorrow, and tomorrow than later.' Aware of the dangers entailed in that proposed journey through enemy territory, he asked Jeanne if she proposed setting out in the clothes she was wearing. When she replied that she would prefer to wear men's clothes, Jean de Metz got her some from his own servants. She must have discussed the question of clothes with others also, because on her return from the visit to the Duke of Lorraine, she found that some citizens had brought a selection of male garments and shoes to the house where she was lodging. They had also bought another horse for her – she now owned three horses of varying quality.

The royal commander of the city, Robert de Baudricourt, at last gave in to the pressure from all sides and agreed, still with some reluctance, to send Jeanne to the city of Chinon where the Dauphin was presently living. He provided her with an escort comprised of the willing Jean de Metz, and another slightly older squire, Bertrand de Poulengy, who had known Jeanne and her parents in their own village – he would later testify that they were good workers and that Jeanne was a devout young girl, almost like a saint, who often cared for her father's cattle and horses. In addition to the letter he had already sent to the Dauphin at Chinon, both Jean and Bertrand would have been instructed by Robert de Baudricourt to report personally to the Dauphin and his counsellors all that was known of Jeanne's behaviour since her first coming to Vaucouleurs. Each of these noble squires had a soldier-servant. Two other men made up the party of six to accompany Jeanne, one named Colet de Vienne, a royal messenger – he would be professionally familiar with all the highways and byways but he would also be able to tell them which towns or cities were hostile – and finally, a soldier named Richard Larcher.

Before allowing Jeanne to depart, however, Robert de Baudricourt did something that showed how he still felt unsure about this girl and her divine mission to save France. Like all Christians, he believed that good and evil influences are operative on the soul; he also, like all Christians of his time, was very much aware of the tribunals of the Inquisition whose job it was to protect the church from heretics and the influence of evil spirits manifested in such things as magic and witchcraft. As a prudent man, he decided that he might need to defend himself if it should turn out that this girl, Jeanne, was not inspired by God but by the powers of evil. To this end, he arrived one day at the house where Jeanne and Durand Laxart were lodging with a couple named Le Royer. He brought with him the parish priest of Vaucouleurs, Jean Fournier. Wearing his stole, the priest declared that he had come to pronounce an exorcism on Jeanne. She went up to him and knelt before him, having no option but to submit to the ritual; later, however, she complained to her hostess, Catherine Le Royer, that the priest had done a foolish thing – she had already been to Confession to him, she said, and he knew well that she was a good and faithful Christian who was not in need of any such ritual of exorcism.

Perhaps to make amends, on the day when they set out from Vaucouleurs, Robert de Baudricourt, as commander of the city, went with Jeanne and her escort as far as the gate leading to the west and Chinon; there, he sent them officially on their way with the rather ambiguous valediction, 'Va, va, et advienne que pourra!' (Go, go, and happen what may!). At last, nine months after her first appearance in Vaucouleurs, Jeanne la Pucelle was on her way to meet the Dauphin of France.

CHAPTER FOUR

The Peasant meets the Prince

The journey from Vaucouleurs to Chinon would take eleven days on horseback, six through the hostile Burgundian territory as far as the town of Sainte Catherine-de-Fierbois where French control began, and a further five to Chinon. During the first part of the journey, they travelled mostly by night in order to avoid roaming bands of Burgundian or English troops. The five military men who accompanied Jeanne on that long ride, during which they often slept in the fields, were deeply impressed by two things about her; firstly, they were astonished at her physical endurance and her ability to ride as well as themselves – others had been surprised by this, unaware of the experience peasant girls like Jeanne could have in dealing with the family's horses; secondly, her personal piety, evidenced in her desire to hear Mass – it was impossible during the first stage of the journey. Her decorous behaviour and conversation made the journey unique in the experience of men who were used to the loose moral standards of courtesans and camp followers. Years later, they testified that they began to feel involved in this great mission she talked about so fervently and that there seemed to be an aura of holiness about her that prevented them from feeling any carnal desires towards her.

As soon as they arrived at the safe town of Sainte Catherine-de-Fierbois, Jeanne dictated a letter to the Dauphin, asking him to receive her. This would have been carried to Chinon by the royal messenger, Colet de Vienne, who was one of the group. She was also able to hear Mass, probably accompanied by her military escort even if some of them had become personally negligent in that observance. The second stage of the journey was without danger from enemy soldiers but still involved five days of rough travel. On 4 March 1429, Jeanne and her escort arrived at Chinon, where she took lodgings in a hostel while the two noble squires, Jean de Metz and Bertrand de Poulengy made official contact with the royal court. When we recall how Jeanne had been invited to visit the Duke of Lorraine even while she was still waiting at Vaucouleurs for Robert de Baudricourt to help her, it can be assumed that rumours about this strange girl and her claims had reached the Dauphin long before he received the official letter from the royal commander of Vaucouleurs or the corroborative personal messages from Jeanne's two noble escorts. In all of those reports, the Dauphin and his counsellors would have taken note of Jeanne's insistence that he could expect no help from any other source. The churchmen in the royal entourage would note especially the report of the precautionary exorcism at Vaucouleurs, an item the commander would have been careful to include in his letter.

The Dauphin was too cautious a man to allow this daring peasant girl from a far-off village into his presence without instigating some preliminary testing by his own counsellors. During the next two days, apart from the curiosity of the general public, Jeanne had to endure visits and interrogation about herself and her so-called divine mission from the agents of the Dauphin himself. Their report was not unanimous; some, judging her to be obviously mad and suffering from hallucinations, advised the heir to the throne of France to get rid of her at once, while others reacted like the men who had been her escort on the long journey from Vaucouleurs – impressed by her personality and sincerity, as well as by the perseverance she had already shown and the hardships she had endured, they thought the Dauphin should at least listen to her and judge for himself.

On the evening of Sunday, 6 March 1429, Jeanne was summoned to meet the man for whom she had already risked her life – she would do so again many more times in the coming year. That historic meeting has become one of the set pieces in the many plays and films made about Jeanne d'Arc during the centuries since her death at the stake in the market-place at Rouen on 30 May 1431. More powerful than film or theatre, the human imagination can vividly conjure up that moment when the peasant girl from Domrémy, looking more like a young man because of her male attire, walked into the great hall of the castle at Chinon and saw hundreds of richly dressed noble men and women of France gathered in the light of torches and candelabra. What they saw and thought we can also imagine. The Dauphin had decided to make his own test of Jeanne's claim to be sent to him with instructions from a supernatural source. Instead of being seated alone and prominently as royal head of the assembly, he took up a position standing amongst the throng. We are told that Jeanne walked directly to where he was and 'made the curtsies and reverences that are usually made to a king as though she had lived at the court'. She spoke 'with humility and simplicity of manner' and said, 'God give you life, gentle King.' The Dauphin tried to carry on his test, asking her, 'But what if I am not the king?' He pointed out a more imposing figure near him and said, 'There is the king.' To which feeble effort Jeanne replied confidently, 'In God's name, gentle Prince, it is you and none other.'

Several of those present testified later that Jeanne then told the Dauphin why she had come. The friar who was soon to become Jeanne's confessor recorded Jeanne's own version: '*Lorsque le roi la vit, il demanda à Jeanne son nom et elle répondit: Gentil Dauphin, j'ai nom Jeanne la Pucelle et vous mande le Roi des Cieux par moi que vous serez sacré et couronné dans le ville de Reims et vous serez lieutenant du Roi des cieux qui est Roi de France.*' ('As soon as the king saw her, he asked Jeanne her name and she answered: Gentle Dauphin, I am Jeanne the Maid and the King of Heaven orders you through me that you be anointed and crowned in the city of Reims and that you be the lieutenant of the King of Heaven who is the King of France)'.

The Dauphin and his counsellors, as well as all present in that great hall, must have been impressed by the demeanour of this peasant girl, comprising boldness without arrogance, confi-

dence devoid of brashness or complacency, and a natural court-
esy combined with the sincerity of a child; they were even more
impressed at the manner in which she had singled him out. That
much in itself might not have convinced Charles to keep this
strange girl in Chinon for further interrogation. What apparently
caused him to do so was what happened when he arranged to
speak privately with her. Jeanne's confessor, Friar Jean Pasquerel,
tells us what transpired in that conversation: 'The king said to
his courtiers that Jeanne had told him a certain secret that only
he and God knew or could know; and that is why he then had
great confidence in her.' Other sources confirm that story, and
inevitably it has given rise to all sorts of speculation by historians as to the nature of the secret in question; a secret, however, it
has remained. Whatever its nature, the Dauphin took Jeanne's
knowledge of it as a sign that she and her message to him were
to be treated with care and caution.

The caring part of this treatment saw Jeanne being placed in
the personal keeping of the wife of Guillaume Bellier, head of
the royal household. Unlike poor Mozart some centuries later,
lodged with the servants by the major-domo of the Archbishop
of Salzburg, Jeanne was allocated royal quarters in one of the
many towers of the great castle of Chinon. A boy of fifteen,
Louis de Contes, was appointed to her service as her personal
page. He testified later that men of high rank often came to con-
verse with her, and women were with her at night; also, that he
had often seen her on her knees praying, and sometimes weeping, he did not know why. Perhaps Jeanne's heavenly voices
were preparing her for the ordeals to come.

The cautionary aspect of the Dauphin's treatment of the girl
from Domrémy was twofold. The first was practical and short.
As has been explained, by consistently using the title, la Pucelle,
Jeanne was making a public declaration of her mission as that of
a virgin consecrated to the service of God and acting under divine guidance. The Dauphin, probably on the advice of his royal
counsellors, decided that the first essential was to ascertain
whether her claim to be a virgin were genuine; if it should turn

out to be false, she would be at once discountenanced and rejected as a liar and a false prophet. Two noble ladies were appointed to carry out the investigation. Their report was positive; the girl was making no false claim in her title.

The second part of the cautionary approach was more tedious and involved; it concerned Jeanne's assertion that she was the agent of divine assistance that would gain the throne of France for its rightful king. To examine this or any other assertion about divine assistance, the Dauphin turned to the ecclesiastical personages among his counsellors.

Among the many knights and noblemen who were now meeting up with Jeanne, there was one in particular who became her enthusiastic supporter and comrade in arms. This was John, Duke of Alençon. He was then twenty-three years old, but had only recently returned from England where he had been a prisoner for five years. He was a close relative and confidential friend of the Dauphin. As soon as he heard about the Maid from Domrémy who had arrived at the royal court in Chinon, he came there to see her for himself. He was her table companion with the Dauphin, and recollected walking in the fields with them and seeing Jeanne practising with a lance – he was so impressed with her skill that he made her a present of a horse! It is from this man, whom Jeanne later called 'my fair duke', that we learn that the Dauphin decided that Jeanne should be examined by churchmen. He seems also to have deputised for the Dauphin at the interrogations which consisted of formal questions about her voices and her mission. Later, however, at dinner, Jeanne told him that she knew more than she had told those who had questioned her.

The positive report from this first formal inquiry did not put the Dauphin's mind at ease. He decided on a second and more official interrogation, to take place at the city of Poitiers before a larger and more learned group of theologians and church authorities. To preside over this inquiry, the Dauphin chose the Archbishop of Reims, the city to which Jeanne said she would bring him to be anointed king – after she had driven the English away from Orléans.

To Poitiers, therefore, Jeanne was sent. She was placed in the house of Jean Rabateau, an advocate of the *Parlement* of Paris. Like some of the churchmen from the University of Paris, those theologians before whom Jeanne was to be questioned, he had been forced to leave Paris because of his loyalty to the Dauphin. In spite of the report furnished by the two noble women who had examined Jeanne at Chinon, other women were appointed to watch her behaviour secretly; they found nothing to report except what was known already, that she was personally modest and chaste, devout and regular in her religious practice. Meanwhile, the theologians questioned Jeanne at length over a period of three weeks. The official transcipt of that interrogation has not survived, but there are many references to it and extracts from it in other sources. One of the theologians, a Dominican named Seguin Seguin who later became Dean of the Faculty of Poitiers, recalled in later testimony Jeanne's own account of how her mission was revealed to her; it corroborates that of Jeanne's confessor quoted elsewhere, and it shows that, like the prophet, Jonah, when he was told to go and preach repentance to the people of Nineveh, the young country girl at Domrémy was initially frightened and perturbed at being made aware of a supernatural intervention in her hitherto ordinary life.

'When she was minding the animals,' Friar Seguin testified, 'she became aware of a voice that told her that God had great pity for the people of France, that she herself must go into France (i.e. the area still controlled by the French). When she heard that she began to weep; then the voice told her that she must go to Vaucouleurs, and that there she would meet up with a captain who would guide her safely into France and to the king, and that she should not be in doubt. And that is what she did, and she came to where the king was without any hindrance.'

The Dominican theologian also recalled some of Jeanne's responses – without exception, he says, all were amazed at the manner and content of her speech – which told against himself. 'When I asked her what language her voice spoke, she said:

'Better than yours! Myself,' explains Friar Seguin wryly, 'I spoke the dialect of Limoges.' He got a more upsetting retort when he asked Jeanne if she believed in God, and she replied: 'Yes, I do – better than you.' When another theologian posed the tricky question: 'If God promised you that he will free the people of France from their enemies, what need is there of soldiers?' Jeanne's reply impressed them: 'In God's name the soldiers will do battle, and God will give the victory.' Jeanne grew impatient when she was urged to give more evidence of her mission before the tribunal could recommend that the Dauphin supply her with an army. 'In God's name,' she snapped, 'I did not come to Poitiers to produce signs. Convey me to Orléans and I will show you the sign for which I have been sent.'

This friar also recorded that Jeanne predicted to the tribunal four things that would happen: the siege of Orléans would be lifted, the king would be crowned at Reims, the city of Paris would return to its loyalty to the king, and the Duke of Orléans (then a prisoner in England) would return safely to his city. Giving his testimony many years later, Friar Seguin concludes: 'And all these things did come to pass as she predicted.'

Another commentator, Jean Barbin, an advocate of the *parlement*, summed up the impression Jeanne made on that assembly of lawyers, bishops and theologians, and the result of the long interrogation: 'They marvelled at her responses and believed that there was something of the divine in them, considering the circumstances of her life and her character; finally, it was concluded as a result of their questioning and investigation that there was nothing evil in her and nothing that was contrary to the Catholic faith; and that, seeing the great necessity in which the king and the kingdom now found themselves – the king and his subjects being at that moment in despair and having no hope of help unless it came from God – the king should make use of her assistance.' With regard to Jeanne herself, the report to the king said: 'We find nothing evil in her, but only good, humility, virginity, devotion, honesty and simplicity.' The testimony of her hosts at Poitiers, Jean Rabateau and his wife, added a personal and more intimate observation. They said that every day after dinner, and also during the night, Jeanne prayed on her knees for a long time, and that she often went to a little chapel in the house and prayed there for a long time.

A man much more cautious and fearful than the Dauphin could not but be convinced by now, considering the combined weight of evidence from his advisers, that this girl from Domrémy was neither evil nor mad; the noble ladies who had examined her physically assured him that the significant title she awarded herself, Jeanne la Pucelle, was valid, while his learned theologians could find no fault with her orthodoxy. But the final test awaited her. She had repeatedly asserted that, with God's help, she would first raise the siege of Orléans and then bring the Dauphin to Reims to be crowned. The Dauphin and his council were now about to send her to Orléans, a city almost entirely surrounded by the English who had so far resisted all the efforts of the French to drive them away. Whether this peasant girl from Domrémy would do so was to be the crucial test of her veracity and of the genuineness of her mission.

CHAPTER FIVE

Jeanne becomes a Warrior

Before Jeanne la Pucelle arrived at Orléans to confront the English in person, she informed them by letter of her approach. On Tuesday 22 March of Holy Week 1429, while she was still undergoing interrogation by the theologians at Poitiers, she dictated an extraordinary letter in which she boldly addressed the boy King of England, his uncle and regent, the Duke of Bedford, and several of the leading English commanders. Heading her missive with the holy names, Jesus Maria, she called on the English to 'surrender to the Maid, who is sent from God, the King of Heaven, the keys to all of the good cities that you have taken and violated in France'. She told them of her mission, and that the rightful King of France would regain his kingdom in spite of them. She offered them peace and urged all the archers and soldiers to go home safely; otherwise, they would be killed – and she included their French allies in her threats.

In that year, 1429, Good Friday of Holy Week fell on the same date, 25 March, as the Feast of the Annunciation. Such a coincidence was traditionally marked by a special pilgrimage to an ancient shrine of Our Lady at Le-Puy-en-Velay. Some of the party who had accompanied Jeanne on the first stage of her adventure, from Vaucouleurs to Chinon, are known to have gone on that pilgrimage. They met up with pilgrims from Jeanne's own province, including her mother, Isabelle. Both she and they seem to have known a devout priest, Jean Pasquerel, in the Augustinian convent at Tours, where the Dauphin sometimes stayed. Fr Pasquerel would surely have already heard much about Jeanne and her mission. On their return, Jeanne's friends recommended him to her; he became her confessor and principal chaplain to the motley collection of troops comprising the French army. From his later testimony we learn much of her influence on the soldiers and of her active part in the actual fighting.

Now that Charles had accepted the extraordinary development in his fortunes whereby a young peasant girl was to be the commander of his army, he decided that Jeanne la Pucelle should be fitted out in the fashion befitting such a rank. Jeanne was taken to the city of Tours where a famous armourer was paid to make her a suit of armour. Jeanne herself, on the direction of her heavenly counsellors, ordered two standards to be designed, one for herself 'on which was painted the image of Our Saviour,' and another to be carried by the priests who accompanied the army, this latter bearing 'the image of the crucified Lord.' We are told that in the fighting at Orléans, Jeanne 'took the standard in her hand when she went to the assault, so as to avoid killing anyone.'

When her military equipment was to be completed with a sword suitable for a commander – she already had a sword given to her by Robert de Baudricourt of Vaucouleurs when she set off for Chinon – Jeanne refused to have one made. Instead, to the surprise of all, she asked that a messenger be sent to the church at Sainte-Catherine-de-Fierbois, the first town in safe French-controlled territory where she had stayed on her way from Vaucouleurs to Chinon. She dictated a letter for the church authorities there, asking that they kindly give her the sword that was buried behind the altar – it would be found to be rusted, with five crosses engraved on it. An armourer from Tours went on that strange mission and returned with the sword. A year later, on trial for her life before the interrogators at Rouen, Jeanne was asked how she knew that sword would be there although she had never seen it. She knew from her heavenly voices, she said, and added that when the men of the church found it they 'gave it a good rubbing, and the rust fell off completely'. When this sword was brought back to Tours, the clergy there offered Jeanne two ornate sheaths for it; but she, with her innate peasant practicality, ordered a sheath of 'good, strong leather'.

At Tours also Jeanne was provided with the entourage suited to her new eminence as a military commander. This consisted of a steward, two pages, and two heralds. In the ritual of diplomacy and warfare, heralds had an important official function; they wore a distinctive livery, and they were supposed to enjoy immunity from attack when they delivered messages or challenges from opposing armies and rulers. Jeanne was also given the use of several war-horses such as knights rode in battle, as well as other horses for ordinary purposes. Back at her native village, Domrémy, as everywhere else in France, the name and mission of Jeanne la Pucelle had already become the big news item. Two of her brothers, Pierre and Jean, and probably some other young men from the area, came to join her at Tours. This could have left their father, Jacques Darc, short-handed in working his farm and cattle, unless, like the Galilean fisherman father of the brothers, James and John, who were called 'to be fishers of men,' he was of sufficient means to be able to employ hired help. As an important man in the village, Jacques Darc was probably affluent enough to do so, and he apparently offered no objection to the departure of his sons to join the forces now commanded by his teenage daughter.

An unusual feature of the Siege of Orléans consists in the fact that, according to the laws of chivalry which had developed in the Middle Ages through the influence of the Christian religion in western Europe, Orléans should not have been under siege at all. A city whose lord was currently a prisoner of the enemy was supposed to be immune from attack. The Duke of Orléans being still a hostage held to ransom in England since 1415, the English should have refrained from laying siege to the city which was, in effect, the capital of his duchy. The laws of chivalry, of course, had never been of concern or benefit except to the nobles and knights who went into battle on horseback, as the French words indicate: *cheval*, a horse, *chevalier*, a warrior on horseback, a knight. The increasing ferocity of the different phases of the Hundred Years War between England and France – especially the ravages of the undisciplined mercenary troops and lawless banditry – gradually eroded the moral code of warfare as imagined in the tales of King Arthur and other sagas, until it deteriorated into the material for the fantastic stories of gallant knight errants defeating giants and monsters and rescuing fair ladies in distress. A few centuries later, that branch of pulp fiction provided a frustrated playwright, Miguel de Cervantes, with the idea for a comic story about a poor country gentleman, Don Quijote de la Mancha, who was driven crazy by reading such ludicrous yarns and set out to be a knight-errant himself; although its author died in poverty, the pot-boiler now ranks as the classic work of fiction in Spanish literature.

In the enforced absence of its lord, the city of Orléans was defended by his half-brother, John, Count of Dunois, known as the Bastard of Orléans – such a title was a common one in times when the illegitimate children of kings and nobles were treated as the equals of 'honest Madame's issue', as Shakespeare phrased it in *King Lear*, in all but the right of succession. Dunois, as he was also commonly known, had been reared until the age of ten with the Dauphin, Charles, and he became one of his most loyal supporters and commanders in the struggle for the restoration of the kingdom. In the early years of the current phase of the war, he had himself been a prisoner of the Burgundians for two years, and even before the English arrived to lay siege to Orléans, he had been charged with the onerous task of trying to raise the huge ransom demanded for the release of his half-brother, Duke Charles. It is in a letter written by Dunois in February 1429, from his besieged city, soon after Jeanne la Pucelle set out on her mission, that historians glean the first documentary mention of her. So significant a historic statement is worth quoting in the original: *'On dit qu'une pucelle est passée par la ville de Gien, qui se rend auprès du noble Dauphin pour lever le siège d'Orléans et pour conduire le Dauphin à Reims pour qu'il soit sacré'* ('It is said that a maid has passed through the city of Gien, who presented herself to the noble Dauphin to raise the siege of Orléans and to bring the Dauphin to Reims to be anointed').

Perhaps because his situation was becoming increasingly desperate as the English continued their methodical encirclement of the city, and there seemed to be little hope of a relief force arriving from any source, Dunois did not dismiss this strange news lightly, but sent messengers to the Dauphin's court to find out more about this Maid and her declarations. In the meantime, he continued with the task in hand, the defence of the city until help arrived, whether by natural or supernatural means, to drive the English away. The English had now been seven months in position around Orléans, having arrived in the previous October. Their temporary forts were blocking all access to Orléans except the road from the east. They also controlled the south bank of the Loire. The only bridge from the city to this southern bank crossed a small island in the river to the strong fort known as Tourelles which had been abandoned by the French. They had also, as had been done in previous wars, destroyed the Augustinian church adjacent to that fort so that it could not be used to house troops or as a source of attack. It was at the fort of Tourelles that the English suffered a setback at the commencement of the siege when their commander, the Earl of Salisbury, surveying the city across the Loire from a window in that vantage point, was killed by a stone fired from a cannon on the walls of Orléans. The French regarded his death as an act of divine retribution for the unchivalrous attack on Orléans, while the English went on with the siege under a new leader, John Talbot, who arrived in December with more troops and bombards as the cannon were called.

The fighting during the seven months since the arrival of the English had consisted mainly in bombardment of the city which damaged houses but did not cause many fatalities – the projectiles in use were heavy stones, the high explosive shell not having been invented yet by the geniuses who think up such devices of mass slaughter. They made a probing attack in January near one of the city gates, but were repulsed. Meanwhile the garrison made several sorties, usually to protect the arrival of provisions, and they actually took a few prisoners. Reinforcements for both sides arrived in early 1429, John Fastolf with over 1,000 for the besiegers, and John Stuart, constable of Scotland, with about the same number of Scots to raise the spirits of the citizens.This John Stuart was the son of the Duke of Albany, regent of Scotland, who was then a prisoner in England. He had arrived in France in 1420, together with William Stuart, Earl of Buchan, and 6,000 Scottish troops. Another indication of the close alliance between France and Scotland was the fact that the Bishop of Orléans at this time was a Scot, John of Kirk-Michael (known in France as Jean de Saint-Michel).

The most serious encounter between the English and the French before Jeanne arrived at Orléans took place in February 1429. Word reached the Bastard Dunois that a great convoy of wagons and carts had set out from Paris to bring supplies of food and weapons to the English at Orléans. If it arrived, the English would be able to continue their encirclement of the city and intensify the bombardment. Dunois decided to intercept and destroy the convoy. Unlike a similar foray by Patrick Sarsfield in 1690, when he led a body of cavalry to intercept and destroy the cannon and supplies en route from Dublin to the city of Limerick, then under siege by William of Orange, the result was a disaster for Dunois. The French suffered a heavy defeat in which they lost over 400 men, including the Scot, William Stuart, and many other nobles. Dunois himself was wounded in the foot and only escaped with his life because two of his soldiers helped him back on to his horse. As the main item of food in the convoy consisted of barrels of salted herring, the English mockingly named the encounter the Battle of the Herrings. A few days after that disaster, most of the notable people in Orléans, obviously giving up hope of relief, left the city – they included the Archbishop of Reims and the Scottish Bishop of Orléans, as well as some of the commanders with their troops. The worried citizens were told that the reason for this departure was to discuss the siege with the Dauphin at Chinon, and that the troops would return with supplies and reinforcements. Only the Bastard Dunois and another commander, with their own troops, were left in the city.

The citizens of Orléans then sent a deputation to the Duke of Burgundy, Philip the Good, an ally of the English, to take the city under his protection while their own lord, the Duke of Orléans, was a prisoner in England. When the English regent, the Duke of Bedford, suspicious of his French ally's ambitions, refused to agree to this settlement, Burgundy withdrew his troops from the English forces besieging Orléans. The situation inside the walled city worsened from then on as the English continued their systematic construction of bastides with the object of blocking all supplies and reinforcements. No wonder, then, that Dunois took such an interest in the news about the Maid from Domrémy. Further news about her reached him and the citizens in April, this time of a more definite and practical kind – she had been accepted as genuine by the Dauphin and she was now assembling a great army at Blois, a fortified city on the Loire, to come to the relief of Orléans.

The army assembling downriver at Blois was joined by some of the lords and commanders who had left Orléans, including the Archbishop of Reims and a renowned soldier of fortune, Étienne de Vignolles, known as *La Hire* because of his wrathful character, who would prove to be one of Jeanne's most loyal and devoted generals. To commanders and soldiers alike, Jeanne stressed that the campaign was a crusade under the direction of heaven. Not only her confessor, who went everywhere with the army, but nobles like the young Duke of Alençon, testified later that she forbade pillage and blasphemy, exhorted the soldiers to confess their sins before battle, and drove away the unfortunate prostitutes who were an accepted part of every army then and for long after. The Duke of Alençon himself, as well as the rough-tongued La Hire, were rebuked personally by La Pucelle when she heard them swear. The extraordinary aspect of it all is that noble lords, hardened mercenary soldiers, and the common troops, all alike tried to conform to these moral directions from a young peasant girl who now seemed to them to be truly sent by God to turn the tide of battle and bring the rightful King of France to his throne. On the other hand, the English were convinced that this young woman dressed in armour and leading an army must be a witch who, by the power of Satan, had duped the gullible French into believing that she would win the war for them by magic.

Jeanne's confessor, Friar Jean Pasquerel, has left a vivid description of the day when the army finally set out from Blois and its progress to Orléans:

> When Jeanne left Blois to go to Orléans, she had all the priests gather round the standard, and then the priests went before, leading the army. They marched out in that fashion, and they sang *Veni Creator Spiritus* and many antiphons. They camped in the fields that night and the next day also. On the third day, they arrived near Orléans, where the English had set up their siege along the bank of the Loire. The king's soldiers and the English came so close that they could see one another within easy reach. And the food supplies were brought there by the soldiers of the king.

It was Friday 29 April 1429. Jeanne la Pucelle had finally reached Orléans where the first part of her promise to the Dauphin Charles was to be put to the test.

CHAPTER SIX

In the Heat of Battle

When Jeanne set out with her priest-led army from Blois she believed that they were going to encounter the English forces in a pitched battle that would end in victory for the French and the departure of the surviving English from the area around Orléans. When, after three days' march, she saw the walls of the besieged city for the first time, she had not even seen any English troops. Instead of leading her into a direct conflict with the English, the military men who had accepted her as an inspiring heaven-sent leader for the troops had decided, in their own pragmatic terms, that further reinforcements and supplies – most of the latter, including livestock, were still in ships at Blois, awaiting a favourable wind to sail upriver to Orléans – would be necessary before a full-scale battle could be attempted. The main object of the Bastard Dunois was to bring more supplies to his beleaguered city. The route to Orléans, therefore, had been a circuitous one, avoiding contact with the English in their forts and encampments, and with the intention of approaching Orléans from the east, where the road to the Burgundy gate was the only one still not blocked by an English bastide.

When Dunois, the commander of Orléans, judged that Jeanne and her force were nearing the city, he staged a diversionary surprise attack on one of the English forts in order to distract the enemy's attention from the troops and supplies coming with Jeanne. The Bastard of Orléans and Jeanne la Pucelle met together for the first time shortly after that successful sortie – the French had returned with some prisoners and an English standard – but if he thought she was going to praise him for his efforts, the royal commander of Orléans was in for a shock. He recalled the conversation vividly in later life, and must often have recounted it down through the years.

'Are you the Bastard of Orléans?'

'I am, and I am very glad at your coming here.'

'Are you the one who gave the orders that I should come this way, on this south side of the river, and not go straight to give battle to Talbot and the English?'

One can imagine the open mouth of this royal commander, a veteran of many battles – and still limping from his wound on the 'Day of the Herrings' – at being spoken to in such terms by this young woman in her shining new armour who had never even seen a dead soldier. When he found his speech, he tried to initiate her into military strategy.

'I explained to her that I and others, including the wisest men with me, had given this advice, because we believed it to be the best and the safest.'

Jeanne la Pucelle then gave him an insight into a strategy not to be found in military counsels or by experience on the battle-field. 'In God's name, the counsel of Our Lord is wiser and safer than yours. You thought that you could fool me, and instead you have fooled yourself. I bring you better help than ever came from any soldiers to any city; it is the help of the king of heaven.'

Dunois then pointed out to Jeanne that, although some supplies had come with her advance army, there were still more troops being gathered at Blois; also – and this was his principal worry – that the great convoy of essential supplies, still in the ships downriver at Blois, could not sail against the current because of the strong wind that was blowing from the east for several days. His own account goes on: 'At that very moment, the wind suddenly changed to the opposite direction and was in favour for the ships to bring the supplies to the city.' His conclusion gives us an insight into the effect Jeanne had on many others of his kind: 'From that moment I had great hope in her, more than ever before.'

Jeanne, however, had learned her lesson. From then on, she did not trust the military commanders but made her own deci-

sions based on the strategy taught her by her heavenly counsellors, a strategy she had explained to her interrogators at Poitiers
earlier: 'The soldiers will do the fighting – and God will give the
victory.' For the present, no fighting could be done. Dunois
urged Jeanne to allow him to bring her troops back to Blois
where the Loire was fordable and where they would join up
with the reinforcements gathering there; meanwhile, he and the
civic authorities of Orléans begged her to enter the city in order
to raise the spirits of the citizens. She agreed reluctantly, and the
ensuing processional entry into a city that had for seven months
been expecting marauding English attackers to come over the
walls can be imagined from the account in the contemporary
Journal of the Siege of Orléans:

> And so Jeanne la Pucelle entered the city, with the Bastard
> of Orléans at her left, very richly armed and mounted;
> then came the other lords and nobles, with squires, cap-
> tains, and men-at-arms, as well as some of the garrison
> and city officials who had gone out to meet her, also men-
> at-arms, carrying torches and all rejoicing as if they had
> seen God himself descend among them ... They felt al-
> ready comforted, as if freed from the siege by the divine
> virtue that they were told resided in that simple Maid ...
> and there was a great crowd, men and women and little
> children, all pressing to touch her or the horse on which
> she rode.

With her entourage, which now included her two brothers,
Jeanne was lodged in the house of the most important civic official in the city, Jacques Bouchard, treasurer of the absent Duke of
Orléans. Next day, she went out to inspect the defences of the
city and to survey the English positions on the other side of the
river. At one point, she engaged in a verbal exchange, shouting
to a group of the enemy that they should go away in God's name
or she would soon come and drive away any of them that survived the attack. A French renegade commander, the Bastard of
Granville, shouted back that she hardly expected them to sur-

render to a woman, adding lewd personal insults to Jeanne and some disparaging remarks about her French troops. In the evening, she went to the ramparts overlooking the only bridge connecting the city with the south bank across an island in the river. Two arches of the bridge had been destroyed by the defenders. At the far end stood the fort of the Tourelles with a strong garrison under the command of Glasdale, an experienced English lord. He and Jeanne exchanged words – they must have agreed, by means of heralds, to such a parley – and she again urged him and his troops to surrender, promising that their lives would be spared. Glasdale and his soldiers replied with insults, calling her a peasant and a cowgirl. Glasdale added the threat that if ever they got hold of her they would burn her. That threat would be fulfilled in due course, but Glasdale himself was destined to die within days at the spot where he made it.

The next day, Sunday 1 May, Jeanne was again put on display, riding around the city and greeted enthusiastically by the citizens. Two more days passed, with another procession on the Tuesday to celebrate the Feast of the Finding of the Holy Cross. Jeanne waited in frustration for the return of Dunois, commander of the city, to hear what news he had of the reinforcements and the movement of the army. He finally came on Wednesday 4 May, accompanied by the redoubtable La Hire and some others, and brought the news that a large English force, under the famous commander, John Fastolf, had been reported as heading towards Orléans. In her excitement at the prospect of a battle at last, Jeanne warned him – as he later testified – that if he did not keep her correctly informed this time she would 'have his head cut off'. It is to be presumed that he regarded it as a friendly exaggeration.

Jeanne did not have to wait for the great battle she thought was looming. That evening, her steward relates, 'she got up from her bed and woke me with shouts. When I asked her what she wanted, she said, "My voices have told me that I must go against the English, but I don't know if I should attack their forts or attack Fastolf who is coming to support them." While her steward saddled her horse, the wife and daughter of her host helped Jeanne to don her armour, she cried out that French blood was already being spilled. She rode out by the Burgundy Gate and encountered many wounded French soldiers on their way back from a skirmish at the Saint-Loup bastide, the only one the English had so far erected to the east of the city; but she rode on towards the scene of battle where she found that the French who had sortied from the city were now meeting with heavier resistance from the English. As soon as Jeanne appeared on her horse, however, the chronicle tells us, 'the French raised a great shout and took the bastide and fortress'.

This first victory would have been of minor effect in a great campaign, but its significance for the context in which it occurred was very great. It revived the long flagging spirits of the French soldiers and convinced the citizens of Orléans that Jeanne la Pucelle would go on to achieve the greater victory in driving the English away for good. For Jeanne herself, the skirmish at the fort of Saint-Loup on the bank of the river Loire was her first experience of what the Roman poet, Virgil, in the *Aeneid*, calls 'the accursed lunacy of war'. The sight of dead and dying men, the agony of the wounded, caused her 'to grieve mightily,' says her confessor, Jean Pasquerel. 'She wept for all the men who died without confessing their sins. She then went to confession herself, and she once more exhorted all the soldiers to confess their sins and to give thanks to God for the victory he had granted.'

The day after this significant victory was Ascension Thursday and Jeanne observed the feast day as a day of peace on earth. Her confessor records that she said there would be no fighting on that day, nor would she put on her armour, but would observe the feast day by confessing and receiving the Eucharist. She still hoped that the English commanders would choose peace rather than war. Even before she began her campaign, as has been told, she had dictated a letter addressed to the King of England, the Duke of Bedford, and the other English commanders, urging them to leave France. She now sent her two heralds with a similar letter to the English commanders in the Tourelles fort on the opposite side of the river. When one of the heralds failed to return, Jeanne responded by sending another letter, but by a different method. She tied the letter to an arrow and then, having shouted at the English, 'Read this, here is news for you!' she ordered one of her archers to shoot the arrow across to the English. With the usual offer of peace if they withdrew, Jeanne added: 'I sent you letters honestly, but you have kept my herald, Guyenne, with you. I ask you to send him back to me and I will send you some of the men we took in the fort at Saint-Loup – they were not all killed in the fighting.' When Glasdale read the letter, he shouted to his soldiers, and loud enough for Jeanne to hear: 'We have news here from the whore of the Armagnacs!' Armagnac was the area in the South of France which was the ancestral territory of the royal house, and the English used the term as a derogation of the Dauphin and his claim to be king of France.

Her confessor records that Jeanne was upset by such insults and wept. She took refuge in prayer, and later told him that she had received consolation and good news from her Lord in heaven. She also requested him to rise very early next morning as she wished to confess and hear Mass early; she did not tell him why, but he and all of Orléans were in for another surprise on the following day. Having heard Mass and confessed, she dressed in armour and had her horse prepared. When she encountered the governor of the city, Raoul de Gaucourt, Jeanne's steward later reported their heated discussion. The governor ordered Jeanne not to make a sortie that day because the commanders had decided against it. Jeanne replied that she knew it was better to attack another fort that day as they had done a few days earlier, and that this time it should be the fort the English had established at the ruined church of the Augustinians near the big fort of Tourelles on the opposite side of the river. She stressed that the troops were ready for battle and told the governor that, whether he wished it or not, they would follow her and they would gain a victory as they had done at the fort of Saint-Loup.

The great captain, La Hire, agreed with Jeanne. Together they led a force out by the Burgundy Gate and crossed the river on a bridge made from boats. The English abandoned a small bastide on the opposite bank and retreated to the stronger position at the Augustinian church. They turned defence into attack by coming from that fort in such numbers that the French troops halted, finding themselves in the dangerous situation of having the river behind them and a hostile force bearing down on them. It was at this point that Jeanne and La Hire rallied their wavering troops and led the charge against the English who were pushed back with great losses. The French captured the bastide at the Augustinians while the English survivors retreated to the main fort of Tourelles at the bridge. Jeanne left a strong garrison holding the captured bastide and stayed with them for most of the night. Before returning across the river to the city, she must have assured them that their position was secure and that she would send supplies from the city.

This was a greater victory than the first one; but Jeanne soon found that, while it increased the trust of the citizens and the soldiers in her as their heaven-sent saviour, it did not alter the policy of the governor and his council. She was informed that they had decided on no further fighting because their troops were not yet sufficient in number. Because the city was now well fortified and had sufficient supplies, it would be better, they judged, to wait until the king sent reinforcements rather than engage in any further sorties. It is possible also that some of the council were still in contact with the Duke of Burgundy to whom an appeal for protection had been made earlier. Jeanne's reaction was predictable. She again instructed her confessor, Jean Pasquerel, to be up early on the following day, adding the strange request that he keep close to her on the morrow, 'for I shall have much to do, more than I have done up to this – and tomorrow blood will flow from my own body above the breast'. The good friar can hardly have slept soundly that night.

During the night, citizens of Orléans crossed the river in boats laden with food and wine for the soldiers in the captured bastide at the Augustinians. La Hire and other experienced warriors were obviously in agreement with Jeanne – now that the English had successively lost two of their bastides, their confidence would be shaken and a third blow could be decisive. This third blow had as its objective the main fort at the bridge, the Tourelles. This fort had blocked access to the city for the past seven months. Its capture would re-open communication between the strategic city of Orléans and the south of France; it would also be a stunning psychological blow to the English generally. The English were also well aware of the importance of this fort, and they would endeavour to hold it until the reinforcements under John Fastolf arrived at Orléans; but they were in a desperate situation, with the river behind them and the French forces attacking from the base they had established by capturing the bastide at the Augustinians the day before.

So, for the third time in four days, Jeanne, with the valiant La Hire and the Bastard Dunois as her supporting commanders, led her troops into battle. By this time, knights and men-at-arms and common soldiers were all alike so amazed at the courage and endurance of this peasant girl, wearing armour and charging into the heat of battle as if she had been reared to arms as the son of some great lord, that they would have followed her wherever she declared her heavenly voices told her to go.

The battle for the Tourelles fort at the bridge lasted all day. Jeanne's prediction to her confessor came to pass around noon when an arrow pierced through her armour above her breast. She had to be taken from the battle to have the wound treated, weeping with frustration at being even temporarily *hors de combat*, but she was soon back in the fight, encouraging the soldiers with her cries. As the fierce fighting went on hour after hour, the veteran warriors, Dunois and La Hire, realised that the resistance was more than they had bargained for. Dunois told Jeanne that he was going to order a retreat to the city, back by the way they had come. Her response was predictable. She suggested a break in the assault in order to let the men rest and eat. He agreed reluctantly, and then was astonished to see Jeanne mount her horse and ride to a vineyard some distance away. He and the others could see her dismount there and kneel in prayer. 'She prayed there for about a quarter of an hour,' he recalled. When the fighting resumed – the English in the fort were probably as glad of the break for food and drink as were the attackers – Jeanne took her standard from her squire and 'waved it about in such a manner,' her steward said, 'that all the soldiers thought she was giving a signal and they all rallied to her and with fierce endeavour attacked the breastwork and the bastide.' It was the final act of the battle. The English surrendered. Apart from those killed in the fighting, many had been forced into the river and drowned, including the commander Glasdale – his head-to-toe suit of armour was obviously much heavier than whatever the Roman warrior, Horatius, wore when he swam the Tiber after his heroic stand against the Etruscans. This was the man who had shouted lewd insults at Jeanne and threatened to burn her alive if he captured her; but her reaction to the news of his death was to weep and pray for his soul and for all the other men who had drowned or died in the battle.

The victorious French placed planks cross the arches of the bridge that had been destroyed as part of the defence of the city. As they crossed, they were met by some of the jubilant citizens and soldiers coming from the city. For the first time in seven months, communication between Orléans and the road to the south was open. The capture of the Tourelles fort meant, in effect, that the siege of Orléans was lifted. The chronicler of the siege describes the joy and relief in the city: 'All the priests and the people of the city sang the *Te Deum* and rang all the bells of the churches, thanking Our Lord for this glorious divine consolation. They expressed joy in every manner, and gave wondrous praise to their gallant defenders, and above all others to Jeanne la Pucelle.' Jeanne herself, we are told, spent the night in the fields on the south bank of the river, with all her commanders and men-at-arms, to guard the fort of Tourelles and to be ready for any counter-attack from the English in the other bastides. No attack came, and later in the night Jeanne was brought back to the city to have more treatment of her wound. She was to have little time to rest and recover.

Early next morning, the watchers on the ramparts reported that the English had not gone away. They had gathered all their garrisons from the various bastides still in their possession and they were now massing in battle formation. Jeanne and her commanders quickly assembled their own weary forces and went out to take up a position facing the English. The date was Sunday 8 May, and it was to become a historic one in the annals of both France and England. As it was a Sunday, Jeanne ordered that no attack was to be made – her noble knights and mercenary commanders, as well as the common soldiers, were by now well used to her religious and chivalric attitudes – but if the English attacked them they were to fight bravely. She assured them that they would have the victory. For an hour, the two armies stood face to face only a short distance from the ramparts of Orléans; but the English seem to have accepted that they would only suffer another defeat if they attacked an army led by this woman – or witch – in white armour. To the surprise and relief of the citizens watching from the ramparts, but perhaps disappointingly for the now confident French knights and soldiers, the English were seen to march away in good order. The pen of the chronicler must have raced across the page as he wrote: 'La Pucelle and the other commanders and men-at-arms came back into the city and there was great rejoicing of priests and people, rendering humble thanks to Our Lord for the great victory against the English, ancient enemies of the kingdom. And on that day and the next, the clergy made a great procession along with the lords and captains and the citizens.'

From French and English sources alike the news of the relief of Orléans spread, first to the cities of France, then all over Europe. The name of the girl from a small village in Lorraine, Jeanne la Pucelle, a name unknown to the royal commander when she arrived a year earlier at the city of Vaucouleurs to ask his assistance in her mission, was now spoken with awe in royal and military circles everywhere in Europe. Her exploit in raising the siege at Orléans in three days of battle must have seemed incomprehensible to those who had believed the cause of the Dauphin Charles to be on the verge of collapse as the English and their Burgundian allies pushed farther into what was left of his territory. Inevitably also fantastic legends began to circulate about the childhood and youth of this miraculous Maid as they always did about heroes and saints in those ages when such tales were a standard part of folklore.

The news reached the Dauphin at Chinon on the day after the battle. He expressed his joy and relief by dictating letters to all the cities of France still loyal to his cause. A day later, on 10 May, a messenger on horseback arrived in Paris with the news for the Duke of Bedford, regent of England and commander of the English forces in France. The clerk of the Paris *Parlement* recorded the bad news in his register, making special mention of 'a maid all alone who held her banner between the two enemy forces, according to what is said'. He was so taken with the story of this Maid that in the margin of his page he drew a simple little sketch of a long-haired girl in a dress, with a standard and a sword, the first of many such attempts by artists and sculptors in future centuries to create an image of what that warrior maiden might have looked like.

The Maid of Orléans, as she was to become known in years to come, did not delay in the city to enjoy the celebrations that probably went on for a long time. With John, Count of Dunois, the Bastard of Orléans, she set out to meet the Dauphin at Loches, arriving there on 11 May, only three days after the ending of the siege. She had fulfilled the first part of her mission and she was eager to begin the next stage that would see the Dauphin crowned King of France at Reims.

CHAPTER SEVEN

The Road to Reims

Before her victory at Orléans, Jeanne had encountered problems with the governor and council of that city when they advised caution and delay instead of the direct military action she favoured. Now she was to come up against the same obstacle, but at the much higher and more powerfully obstructive level of the royal council to whom the Dauphin looked for advice. To the members of that council, lay and ecclesiastic, her stated purpose, to bring the Dauphin to Reims to be crowned, was both premature and foolhardy. The city of Reims was traditionally the city in which the King of France should be crowned – the holy oil of consecration was kept there in the Abbey of Saint Rémi – but Reims was situated in that northern third of France under English and Burgundian control. Like most cities in that territory, it was more loyal to the Duke of Burgundy than to the English. Before the Dauphin could go there in safety, another campaign would have to be fought in order to bring the fortified cities of the region into allegiance to the rightful heir to the throne.

The Dauphin himself, while eager for the coronation that would proclaim him the legitimate heir to the throne, was also eager to make peace with the powerful Duke Philip of Burgundy and detach him from his alliance with the English. The feud between the houses of Burgundy and the royal house of Valois originated in two assassinations, firstly when Philip's father, Duke John of Burgundy, caused the murder in 1407 of the present Dauphin's uncle, Louis of Orléans, and subsequently when that foul deed was avenged in similar fashion in 1419 by the death of Duke John himself, treacherously slain under cover of a peace parley. The Dauphin Charles was tormented by guilt for many years because of his own indirect implication in that affair. He was also, of course, aware that Duke Philip of Burgundy, who was lord of very large areas of France as well as of the territory north of France which now comprises Belgium and Holland, might be entertaining the ambition of getting the crown of France for himself by letting the English and the French wear out their resources and then seizing his opportunity.

Meanwhile, there were other influences at work, unknown even to the Dauphin himself, in the diplomatic intrigues between the English and both parties in France.

In her vision of proceeding directly with the military campaign to clear the way to Reims, Jeanne was not aware of the extent and complicated nature of those diplomatic activities by vested interests on all sides of the political triangle in France. She was impatient to continue the fight against the Anglo-Burgundian alliance. While the military commanders like the Bastard of Orléans and La Hire agreed with her view that the war should go on, they thought the campaign should be directed first towards Normandy, where there was growing dissent and even partisan activitiy against the English, and then to the taking of Paris, before the king could be crowned at Reims. Jeanne insisted that her heavenly counsellors should be listened to and that the symbolic coronation should take precedence because it would inspire the whole people of France to proclaim their loyalty to their legitimate king; then, with such popular enthusiastic support, the English would be driven out of France altogether. She argued her case even in the king's own council, and eventually the Dauphin sided with her against them; but he appointed the young Duke of Alençon, whom Jeanne had met in Chinon before she set out for Orléans, to be the overall commander of the new campaign, an indication, perhaps, that he was beginning to worry that Jeanne was becoming too popular.

Duke John of Alençon, one of Joan's most ardent supporters and admirers from the moment he met her with the Dauphin at Chinon, had been unable to take part in the fighting at Orléans because of his knightly word of honour. He had been a prisoner in England, where his father-in-law, the Duke of Orléans, was still held, but had been released on promising not to fight against the English in France until his ransom had been paid in full. This having now been done, he was free and eager to join up with Jeanne in the coming campaign. His young wife, however, was not so keen on an enterprise that might leave her a widow. Jeanne reassured her and promised that she would bring him back safely.

It was a month since the relief of Orléans before the new campaign got under way on 8 June 1429. Jeanne was accompanied by one of her brothers – the other brother may have been needed back at the farm in Domrémy – and the army had increased with many young men, inspired by Jeanne's achievement at Orléans, flocking to the cause from all parts. The first objective was the city of Jargeau to which the English had retreated from Orléans. When the commanders began to argue about attacking the city, now garrisoned by a large Anglo-Burgundian force under the Earl of Suffolk, Jeanne had to remind them once again of the source of her mission. The Duke of Alençon recalled that she told them 'they should not fear the greater number because God would be leading the action. If she were not sure of God's help in the fight, she said she would prefer to be minding the sheep on her father's farm than going into such danger here.'

The English made the decision for them, coming out in force to attack the French troops in the approaches to the city. Once again, Jeanne rode into the battle waving her standard, with the same result as in the previous battles. The English retired into the city as night fell. Next morning, Jeanne urged Alençon and the Bastard of Orléans to assault the city. 'Have no doubt,' she said, 'the hour that pleases God is now.' The Duke also recalled that Jeanne fulfilled her promise to his young Duchess by saving his life at a time in the assault when she told him to move back from the position he was holding or he would be killed by one of the engines firing from the ramparts. He had only moved away when another knight was killed on that very spot. 'That struck great fear into me,' the Duke recalled years later, 'and after that I had great regard for everything Jeanne said.' Jeanne herself did not escape so lightly. She was on a scaling ladder at the walls, her standard in her hand, when a large stone broke her helmet and knocked her to the ground. Before her troops could be disheartened by that sight, she was on her feet, urging them forward to the assault. The city was taken that day, 12 June, and the Earl of Suffolk became a prisoner of the French.

Influenced, perhaps, by the news of the fall of Jargeau to the French, two more cities surrendered when Jeanne and the Duke of Alençon promised the Burgundian garrisons safe conduct. Then the alarming news reached Alençon and Jeanne that a large English army under Talbot and Fastolf was coming to put a halt to their march towards Reims. On 17 June the two armies came in sight of each other at Patay. The coming battle was to be very different from the three attacks on fortified positions by means of which Jeanne had raised the siege of Orléans. This would be a pitched battle in open ground between two formidable forces. The French, under the command of the Duke of Alençon, Jeanne, the Bastard of Orléans, La Hire, and other commanders, numbered about six thousand, and the English something similar. The French, having been given warning by their scouts of the approach of the English, took up a position on a rise and waited for the attack.

On that day, however, there was no fighting. The English sent heralds to make a formal challenge, inviting the French to come down from their position and fight. Jeanne answered for the French that it was late in the day. She advised the English to go and find places to rest, adding, 'tomorrow, with the help of God and Our Lady, we will take a closer look at one another.' During the night, the French got word that reinforcements were arriving for the English, news that caused the worried young Duke of Alençon to consult Jeanne and the other commanders. The Bastard of Orléans recalled that Jeanne's reaction to the Duke's fears was to call out in a loud voice, 'Every one of you have good spurs tomorrow.' Some, including the Duke, thought she was predicting a defeat. 'Do you mean?' they asked, 'that we

are going to turn our backs to the English?' 'No,' she assured
them, 'it is the English who will be defeated; you will need good
spurs to chase after them as they run away.' The Duke of
Alençon recalled that Jeanne said to him before the battle next
day, 'My voices have told me that the king will today have the
greatest victory he has ever had and we shall take a great many
of the English.'

That battle on 18 June 1429 was such a disaster for the
English that it cancelled the advantage gained by the victory of
Henry V at Agincourt in 1415. They lost about 2,000 dead and a
similar number taken prisoner, including their commander,
Talbot. The news of this stunning achievement reached Paris
and struck terror into the citizens. They were convinced that this
all-conquering Jeanne La Pucelle would soon arrive at their
gates with her forces and they began hurriedly to prepare their
defences.

Jeanne's objective, however, was not Paris but Reims. The
Dauphin was now fully in accord with her. While preparing to
set out with the army, he wrote formal letters of convocation to
all the cities in his kingdom and to the peers of France, lay and
ecclesiastical, including his principal native opponent, the Duke
of Burgundy, inviting them to Reims to participate in his coronation. Jeanne also wrote to the Duke of Burgundy inviting him
to come to Reims and swear fealty to the king. The Dauphin then
caused Jeanne further chagrin by delaying his departure. It was
not until 29 June, nearly a fortnight after the victory at Patay,
that he set out with the army on the road to Reims through territory that was still largely under Burgundian control.

One by one the cities on the route altered their allegiance
when their citizens and Burgundian garrisons had to face the
choice between doing so and defending themselves against
what was now a formidable force well equipped with artillery.
The most significant city to submit was Troyes, where the treaty
had been signed after Agincourt that made Henry V regent of
France, gave him the Dauphin's sister as his wife, and proclaimed that his heir was to become king of both countries, thus

effectively depriving Dauphin Charles of his throne. On July 4 the French forces were only a few miles from Troyes. The Dauphin sent a letter to the garrison and the citizens, offering amnesty if they surrendered. Jeanne also sent her heralds with a similar letter: 'Loyal Frenchmen,' she said to the Burgundians inside the ramparts, 'come now before your lord Charles. There is no question of fault, and you need have no fear for your bodies.' Her letter also contained threats of what would happen if they did not surrender, and ended, 'I commend you to God. I expect a swift reply.'

The commanders and city council in Troyes played for time by sending heralds to Reims and Auxerre to find out how the citizens in those citizens would advise them. They also sent envoys to discuss terms with Jeanne and the French army. Among these was a Franciscan friar Richard, who had been driven out of Paris because of his fantastic predictions – he was later to be silenced and locked up by his own order. His inclusion in the deputation is evidence of what the English and Burgundians thought of Jeanne la Pucelle and her astounding victories. Jeanne herself recalled that Friar Richard approached her in the French camp shaking holy water around her and making the Sign of the Cross. She laughed at him and said, 'Be brave, come near me, I promise you I won't fly away!'

As usual, the Dauphin and his counsellors began to prevaricate. The army was now short of food and supplies, awaiting reinforcements. The garrison in Troyes was large and well equipped. As usual, also, Jeanne had no patience with this human approach to her mission. The Bastard of Orléans recollected that she went into the council of the king and urged him to waste no more time in these long discussions, 'for, in God's name,' she assured him, 'in three days I will lead you into the city of Troyes and Burgundy will be astonished by our victory.' She took the initiative without waiting for the Dauphin and his council to come to a decision whether to attack or retreat. When the citizens and the garrison saw her directing the troops to make preparations for the assault, they came to a quick decision themselves and sent envoys to the Dauphin suing for peace. On Sunday 10 July, the Dauphin entered Troyes with great ceremony, and Jeanne, carrying her standard, was by his side.

No other city offered any resistance, but accepted the offer of amnesty and declared their allegiance to the legitimate king of France, Charles VII. At Châlons, Charles, now confident of the success of the campaign, issued a general letter to the whole kingdom, asking the public criers in every town to inform the people that he was on his way to be anointed and crowned at Reims and inviting them to attend – the ritual of coronation was still a public ceremony. The people responded gladly and began to converge on the city of Reims from all directions. Jeanne even met with some people from her native village, one of whom later recalled that, in private conversation, she said that she feared nothing except treason, an ominous sign that her voices may have warned her of what was to come. On 16 July, the Dauphin received a deputation from the city of Reims who offered him total surrender and loyalty. On that same day, certain prominent people hurriedly left the city. They were what Jeanne and others would consider renegade Frenchmen who had sided with the English against the legitimate heir to the throne. Among them was Pierre Cauchon, the Bishop of Beauvais. He was a native of Reims, but had achieved distinction as rector of the University of Paris and one of the principal negotiators, for the English side, of the Treaty of Troyes. His own ambitions linked him solidly with the Duke of Bedford and the English objective of uniting the two kingdoms under Henry VI of England. Hence, he was the inveterate enemy of the Dauphin and of this upstart young woman from Lorraine who was claiming to be sent by God to lead the French army and have the Dauphin crowned at Reims. Although he fled from Reims before Jeanne and the Dauphin entered that city, she was destined to meet him face to face when he would preside over her trial and execution in less than a year.

On the evening of that day, Charles entered Reims amid the acclamations of the citizens – although it was July, they cried,

'Noël! Noël!', the chant traditionally associated with coronations because it was on Christmas Day that Charlemagne was crowned in Rome in 800. Possibly because of the fear that Bedford or the Duke of Burgundy might send a force to prevent it, the coronation was not delayed. On the following day, Sunday 17 July 1429, Charles was anointed and crowned in a ceremony that lacked much of the traditional regalia, most of it having been taken to Paris by the English – it would be used later when the Duke of Bedford brought the boy king, Henry VI, from England to be crowned King of France – but in which the vital element, the holy oil, was used, since the English had neglected to take this from the Abbey of Saint Rémi where it was traditionally kept. Among the great gathering at that historic ceremony were the parents of Jeanne la Pucelle. Jeanne herself stood by the side of the king with her standard. Later, when some querulous voices were raised in complaint about this – why should she, and not other commanders, be in that position of honour – she responded that since her standard had shared in all the pains of battle that led to this hour, it was only right that it now share in the honour of the coronation of the king. Although Philip the Good, Duke of Burgundy, as one of the six lay peers of the kingdom, had been formally invited to the coronation both by the Dauphin and Jeanne, he did not attend. Another absentee was the wife of the Dauphin, Marie of Anjou. When the army set out on the road to Reims, Charles had instructed his wife to go to the safety of the city of Bourges in French-held territory. She would be crowned Queen of France later in Paris, when that city had been added to the list of those that had returned to allegiance to the legitimate king.

Jeanne la Pucelle had now fulfilled the two promises she made when she first appeared at the city of Vaucouleurs, and later when she met the Dauphin at Chinon. In a few days, she had relieved the city of Orléans after it had been besieged for seven months by the English. Two months later, she had brought all the cities under Anglo-Burgundian control back to loyalty to the Dauphin, and she had brought the pusillanimous

Charles himself to Reims where he was anointed and crowned as the legitimate King of France. It would appear, then, that the mission to which she had been guided by heavenly voices was at an end, and that she should now return to her life as a peasant girl in the village of Domrémy in the province of Lorraine on the eastern border of France. Subsequent events suggest that the newly-crowned King Charles VII and his counsellors would have been glad if her voices had thus directed Jeanne la Pucelle back to where she came from; it seems, however, that they had revealed to her that her mission was not yet at an end, that she was to continue the military campaign to drive the English out of France, and that she was not destined to see her native village again.

CHAPTER EIGHT

Betrayal

Even before the coronation at Reims, Jeanne had become a topic of scholarly dispute. The first attack on her came in a pamphlet issued by the theologians and scholars in the University of Paris who were on the side of the English and the Duke of Burgundy. It was answered by Jean Gerson, the most famous scholar of the time, who had been Chancellor of the University of Paris but was ousted because of his support for the French. His defence of Jeanne, whom he had not met, was the last of his works; he died a few days before the coronation. Jeanne was also celebrated by a famous woman poet of the day, Christine de Pisan, who had left Paris when the English entered it and gone to live in a convent where her daughter was a nun. Saddened by the state of the country, she remained silent for years until France was rocked by the victories at Orléans and Patay, followed by the coronation of Charles VII at Reims, all accomplished in the course of a few months by an unknown young woman. In July 1429 she composed her poem of 448 lines, hailing Jeanne, 'simple shepherdess, but more valiant than any man ever at Rome ... Never have we heard anyone tell of such a marvel.' Another writer, Alain Chartier, extolled Jeanne in rhapsodic prose: 'Behold her, she who seems not to have come from anywhere in this world but to have been sent from heaven to raise up the French when they were beaten down to the ground ... O unique virgin, you are the glory of the French nation and of all Christians.'

But Jeanne herself was indifferent to praise or denigration. She had an enthusiastic army ready to march on Paris. What she did not have was the unqualified support of the man for whom she had risked her life on many occasions, for whom she had shed her blood. Now that he was anointed and crowned as the legitimate King of France, Charles seems to have decided that the heroic girl from Domrémy had done all that was needed on her part. From this on, without actually dismissing her altogether, he caused her frustration and discouragement by his vacillation. Two of his principal counsellors, Georges de La Trémoille and Regnault of Chartres, the Archbishop of Reims, were now totally opposed to any further military action. The former, La Trémoille, was head of the royal household and also the king's agent for any matters concerning Burgundy. He had been hostile to Jeanne from the beginnng and a few weeks before the coronation he was already engaged in secret peace negotiations with the Duke of Burgundy. The Archbishop of Reims, the man who anointed the Dauphin as king, and who was restored to his city by the coronation, had acted as president of the tribunal that spent three weeks investigating Jeanne at Poitiers. He then advised the Dauphin in her favour and he supported her military activities, perhaps because his father had been killed in 1418 when the Burgundians took Paris, while three of his brothers were killed at Agincourt. Now, however, he joined La Trémoille in making contact with the Duke of Burgundy and in advising the king to make peace. Neither of them knew that at the same time the Duke of Burgundy was planning with the Duke of Bedford to reorganise their forces for a fresh campaign against the French.

As part of the build-up of the Anglo-Burgundian force, Bedford and his uncle and co-regent, Cardinal Henry Beaufort, dared the wrath of the Pope by diverting an army the Cardinal had raised in England by special tithes, sanctioned by the Pope, to fight in a crusade against the heretical Hussites in Bohemia. The Pope had contributed part of the cost of recruiting and supplying this force, but when it landed at Calais it proceeded not to Bohemia to fight in a religious crusade but to Paris where it would form part of the army being assembled to dethrone the newly-crowned King Charles VII. Like his counsellors, Charles was unaware of the fact that Bedford and Burgundy were only playing for time. Even while still at Reims after the coronation,, he agreed to a truce of fifteen days with agents of the Duke of Burgundy. Meanwhile, the Duke of Burgundy, whose sister, Anne, was Bedford's wife, was being entertained by Bedford with great honour and public spectacle in Paris, where the *Parlement*, the University, and the pricipal citizens promised loyalty to the Regent and the Duke.

While Jeanne and the Duke of Alençon waited impatiently for the king to begin the march to Paris, Charles spent the time going from city to city accepting the allegiance of his loyal subjects. When she met with the king at Château-Thierry, Jeanne asked the only favour she had ever requested, that the inhabitants of her native village, Domrémy, and the neighbouring village of Greux, be exempted from taxation in perpetuity. King Charles VII graciously granted her request, and the exemption lasted up to the reign of Louis XVI, ending with the French Revolution in 1789. Jeanne was beginning to sense that some powerful people must be working against her. The Bastard of Orléans recalled a significant remark of hers at this time, while they tried to keep an idle and disgruntled army in readiness for progress towards Paris: 'I wish it would be the will of God my creator that I now give up arms and return to help my parents by taking care of the cattle with my brother and sister; they would be very happy to see me again.'

The Duke of Bedford, having strengthened the defences of Paris, left the city with a strong force and sent notice to the newly-crowned King Charles VII that he was coming to put a stop to his march towards the capital. In that formal communication, he also accused the King of 'depending on the support of the superstitious and reprobate, and even of that mad and notorious woman who dresses in men's clothes and is of immoral conduct.' This was the image of Jeanne la Pucelle he would later spread throughout Europe when he instigated and supervised her trial for heresy. Bedford's challenge finally brought Charles to forget his diplomatic intrigues for the moment and come to join up with Jeanne and the army.

On 15 August 1429, a month after his coronation at Reims, the new King of France at last found himself facing the English army in the fields near Paris. But, as had happened on the final day at Orléans, after the two armies had spent the entire day under a burning sun and in clouds of dust, for some reason there was no battle. Next day, the English began retreating towards Paris. Charles showed no inclination to pursue them and force a fight. He still believed that he could make peace with the Duke of Burgundy and detach him from his alliance with the English. On that very day his emissaries, led by the Archbishop of Reims, were in the presence of the Duke of Burgundy, offering him whatever terms he desired, including the return of many of the cities the French had taken. A few days later, a Burgundian deputation led by John of Luxembourg arrived at Chécy to meet the king in person. After discussions lasting a week, Charles signed a new truce of four months with Burgundy. The English, on their part, were determined to keep the Duke of Burgundy on their side. Bedford appointed him Governor of Paris and Lieutenant-general of France and later added the counties of Champagne and Brie to his already extensive realm. Further troops were being brought in from England, and envoys were sent to several countries, even to Scotland, in an effort to prevent any further aid from reaching the French.

As had happened at Orléans, Jeanne seems finally to have decided that she must take action on her own. She consulted with the Duke of Alençon, the nominal commander of the army, and they decided to test the defences of Paris with an attack on the suburb of Saint-Denis. The Duke later recalled the cynical opinion in the army at the time: 'All were agreed that she would put the king in Paris – so long as he had nothing to do with it.' After some skirmishes, Jeanne led a direct attack at the Saint-Honoré gate on 8 September. The king, having heard of the move, arrived to see the action but took no part himself. He probably was not near enough to see Jeanne, her standard waving as usual, lead the troops into the ditches near the walls to begin the assault. The fighting lasted all day, and towards sunset

Jeanne was hit by a crossbow bolt in her thigh. She still urged the troops to continue, but as it was nightfall, the weary soldiers withdrew, carrying the wounded La Pucelle to the camp at La Chapelle. Next day, despite her wound, she went to the Duke of Alençon to urge him to continue the attack – he had built a bridge to make the assault easier – but he had bad news for her. The king had sent orders that the bridge be destroyed and no further action taken. A few days later he ordered the army to return to the banks of the Loire. One of Jeanne's commanders remarked, 'More than ever now, we who are in the field lose out to those who are sitting in the king's council.' Those diplomats now advised the king to separate the Duke of Alençon altogether from the influence of Jeanne. After this, she never met him again. Some years later, after enduring further ill-favour from Charles and his counsellors, the Duke of Alençon would actually became an ally of the English in France.

The king's counsellor and Jeanne's most inveterate enemy, La Trémoille, arranged that she be kept in the watchful care of his half-brother, the Lord of Albret, who in his turn had her lodged in the city of Bourges at the house of René de Bouligny, the general supervisor of the royal finances. She spent three weeks there, and in later testimony, the lady of the house, Marguerite, recalled how impressed she was with Jeanne's piety and purity. She also recalled that when she and others asked Jeanne La Pucelle to touch their rosaries and other pious objects, Jeanne just laughed at them and said, 'Touch them yourselves – your touch will do as much good as mine!' At this time also a strange visitor came to Jeanne, sent to her by none other than the unbalanced Friar Richard who had shaken holy water at her before she entered the city of Troyes. Catherine de La Rochelle was well suited to be an associate of the crazy Friar. She claimed to have visions during Mass when God revealed great secrets to her. She now told Jeanne that every night a lady dressed in gold was appearing to her with a message for the king – she was to tell him where he would find hidden treasure that would finance his armies. Jeanne watched for two nights with her and then ad-

vised her to go home to her husband and children. She also dictated a letter to the king telling him of her verdict on her weird
visitor.

Having separated Jeanne from the Duke of Alençon and her
other commanders, the scheming La Trémoille now advised the
king to keep La Pucelle busy with military action but only in a
minor way that would not harm the peace moves with the Duke
of Burgundy. She was ordered to attack a powerful man who
was loyal to no side in the triangular affairs of France at that
time. The troubled state of the country had resulted not only in
savage mercenary troops inflicting terror and devastation, but in
some local warlords ruling their territories without regard to
any higher authority. From their castles and fortified towns they
not only put the local population under tribute but also captured
and held to ransom anyone, lord or bishop or merchant, unfortunate enough to come within range of their predatory raids.
One of the most notorious and powerful of these robber barons
was Perrinet Gressart, whose main stronghold was at La-
Charité-sur-Loire. He sold his mercenary aid to the Duke of
Burgundy or to the Duke of Bedford as it suited him. The king's
most influential counsellor, Georges de La Trémoille, had himself fallen victim to the ruthless Gressart, who captured him and
held him until a ransom of 14,000 écus had been paid. Bedford
had recently begun to enlist this bandit chieftain more actively
on the English side by financial and other inducements, as a
result of which Gressart extended his fortified positions and became a serious threat to the French and even to the Burgundian
influence.

A local campaign to subdue a mercenary bandit like Gressart
was not what Jeanne la Pucelle would have chosen, but perhaps
she saw it as a means of keeping some of the king's troops active
while she waited for the major offensive against the English that
would take Paris and compel the English to total surrender. But
even for this diversionary campaign, the king and his counsellors did not supply the necessary troops, equipment and supplies. After one or two minor skirmishes and the capture of one

of Gressart's strongholds. Jeanne had to ask for supplies of food and ammunition from various cities. The main attack, on the central stronghold of La Charité, began on 14 overmber 1429, and had to be abandoned. A contemporary report states the reason bluntly: 'Because the king did not send her supplies or money to maintain her soldiers, Jeanne had to raise the siege and withdraw, at which she was very displeased.'

As if to soothe her and keep her loyal, the king sent Jeanne a letter in December praising her great services and announcing that he was raising her parents and her brothers to the ranks of the nobility. He did not, however, invite her to spend Christmas with him. Instead, she was again under the supervision of La Trémoille in one of the castles belonging to his family. She was, however, invited to a banquet in January 1430 by the city council of Orléans; her brother, who had been with her in all her campaigns, was also present. A week earlier, the Duke of Burgundy married his third wife, Isabelle of Portugal, an alliance that made him even more powerful. He still talked peace with the envoys of Charles, but continued to postpone the proposed peace conference while at the same time demanding the return of the cities taken by Jeanne and preparing for all-out attacks on the French. He was alarmed by the increasing activity of French partisan fighters in Normandy, and even more so by an abortive pro-French rising in Paris itself in March of that year.

While Jeanne and her loyal commanders like La Hire and Dunois, the Bastard of Orléans, still waited in vain for a major campaign against the English, the Duke of Bedford and his ally, the Duke of Burgundy were preparing their own campaign. In the first week of April 1430, the Duke of Burgundy sent his vassal, John of Luxembourg, ahead with a vanguard to a rendezvous point at Péronne, leading out the main army himself a few weeks later. Meanwhile, on 23 April, the Duke of Bedford was at Calais to greet the boy King of England, Henry VI. He had been crowned at Westminster on 6 November, and Bedford was now bringing him to France with the intention of having him crowned King of France in the traditional manner at Reims, thus proclaiming the dual monarchy and challenging Charles VII to defend the legitimacy of his own coronation. Reims, of course, was now in the hands of the French, although it was reported that its citizens were wavering in their loyalty through fear of the Duke of Burgundy. With the boy king, there came from England supplies and reinforcements for the coming campaign. An interesting sidelight on the effect Jeanne's victories had produced on the mentality of the English people is the Duke of Bedford's own revelation that he had been forced on two occasions to send threatening letters to England with instructions to draft men who were refusing to go to fight in France because, they said, they were 'afraid of the artifices of the Maid'.

The movements of two armies, English and Burgundian, in threatening fashion against his territory caused the blinkers to fall from the eyes of the new King of France. Too late, he realised how the Duke of Burgundy had duped him with talk of peace. His chancellor, Regnault of Chartres, Archbishop of Reims, who, along with the other favoured counsellor, La Trémoille, had urged the king to rein in the activities of Jeanne la Pucelle and choose the path of diplomacy instead of war, now acknowledged their mistake. 'After the Duke of Burgundy,' the Archbishop wrote, 'had amused himself and deceived us for a long time with talk of truces and so on, under a pretence of good faith, affirming that he desired to come and make peace, he then set out with his forces to make war against the king, our country, and our loyal subjects.' He makes no mention of Jeanne la Pucelle or of his own opposition to her. If the king had supported her immediately after his coronation, and given her the supplies and troops she requested, he would have been in Paris by now and the English cause would have been in disarray. Instead, Jeanne was now, as she had been in the Autumn, engaged in a futile campaign of inconclusive skirmishes. She had set out in April, with only a few hundred men, to attack some of the Anglo-Burgundian strongholds. Her brother, Pierre, and her faithful steward, Jean d'Aulon, were with her. In contrast to her grand departure for Orléans, with her personal heralds and pages and all the paraphernalia of a royal commander, Jeanne was now little more than the captain of a small group of soldiers, not very different from the mercenary bands that sold their services to the highest bidder.

After a few weeks of sporadic fighting, on 23 May 1430 Jeanne and her small force of about three hundred ran into a large force of Burgundians at Margny near the city of Compiégne. They were part of an army grouped some miles away under the Duke of Burgundy himself. When reinforcements began to arrive from that source, Jeanne and her company had to retreat towards Compiégne. A bridge of boats had been erected to give access to the city across the river Oise. When the retreating French soldiers were crossing the bridge, the commander of the city, Guillaume de Flavy, ordered the drawbridge to be raised. Jeanne, with her brother and her steward and a few others, who were fighting a rearguard action, were left outside, surrounded by the enemy troops. The man whose order to raise the drawbridge left Jeanne in that fatal predicament, Guillaume de Flavy, was a half-brother of Regnault of Chartres, Archbishop of Reims and counsellor of the king. This connection, added to the fact that the gate protected by the drawbridge was not the main city gate in the ramparts but a gate in the outer curtain wall, not vital to the city's defence, has caused many historians to see Jeanne's capture at Compiégne as the fulfilment of her presentiment that she would be betrayed.

A soldier pulled her from her horse and threw her to the ground. They could have killed her on the spot, but the rites of battle in such situations were not about killing but about capture and ransom. The Burgundians knew that they had captured Jeanne la Pucelle, the most famous and feared woman in France. Their captain was Lionel, known as the Bastard of Wandomme, whose lord was John of Luxembourg. He brought Jeanne and the other prisoners back to Margny and sent word of her capture to his own lord and to the Duke of Burgundy. They came quickly to the house in which she was held. There is no record of what transpired at that meeting, but it is easy to imagine with what satisfaction the great Duke contemplated, and probably taunted, the young woman who had caused him and his English allies such trouble. Neither is there any record of how the King of France and his counsellors reacted to the news that the heroine of Orléans, Patay and Reims was now a prisoner in the hands of the enemy. What is known, and it is one of the saddest and strangest facts in the history of France, is that Charles VII allowed Jeanne la Pucelle to remain a prisoner for the next year, which was to be the last year of her life, and made no attempt, with money or by force of arms, to rescue her from the inevitable fate that he and his courtiers knew would be her lot.

CHAPTER NINE

A Woman for Sale

During her subsequent trial, Jeanne stated that, in the course of her last brief campaign in April 1430, she had been forewarned by her heavenly voices, St Margaret and St Catherine, that she would be taken prisoner 'before St John's Day' (June 24). When she asked them when and where, they told her only that she must accept it willingly and that God would aid her. When she asked if, when captured, she would die quickly without long torment in prison, they told her only that 'she should take it all well and it was necessary that it should be so.'

If newspapers and television had existed at the time, the news of the capture of Jeanne la Pucelle by the enemies of the King of France would have been at the top of the headlines. As it was, it spread all over Europe, even to Constantinople, within a few days. The Duke of Burgundy dashed off a letter to all the cities of the realm, as well as letters to rulers in other countries, thanking God for the capture of 'the woman they call the Maid', a capture, he asserted, 'that would show the error and mad belief of all those who were in sympathy with the actions of this woman.'

Three days after the capture of Jeanne, the anti-French lawyers and theologians at the University of Paris wrote to the Duke of Burgundy in terms of most fervent piety and in the name of the Inquisitor of France, calling on him to deliver 'the woman named Joan, whom the adversaries of this kingdom call the Maid' to their jurisdiction 'since she is strongly suspected of various crimes that taste of heresy.' Doubtless, in spite of finding her already guilty of heresy, they would have assured the Pope himself that Jeanne would receive a fair trial according to the strict guidelines laid down by the church.

While such vituperative and vindictive reaction from her enemies could be expected, the manner in which Regnault de Chartres, Archbishop of Reims, wrote to his people in that city concerning the capture of Jeanne is surprising unless we remember the machinations and ambitions of such men who were ecclesiastics, courtiers, and even warriors as the circumstances suited. Jeanne had been hailed by the citizens of Reims as their deliverer from Burgundian control. She stood beside the king when the Archbishop of Reims anointed him at his coronation. Now that she was a prisoner in the hands of the king's enemies, this same archbishop informed the faithful of Reims that this had happened 'because she had become full of pride due to the rich garments she had begun to wear. She had not been doing what God had commanded her, but had followed her own will.' If that was the verdict of the king's counsellor, was it also the convenient view of the king himself and a salve to his conscience in days to come? In order to further convince the people of Reims and elsewhere, Archbishop Regnault found an iconic replacement for Jeanne la Pucelle in the form of a young shepherd boy named Guillaume who, like Catherine de La Rochelle and many others, was seeing visions and hearing heavenly voices in imitation of the peasant girl from Domrémy. The only thing in which that unfortunate boy really compared with Jeanne was that he also would meet with an untimely end.

Jeanne was now a prisoner of John of Luxembourg, whose soldiers had captured her, and he was a vassal of the Duke of Burgundy. In effect, however, she was a commercial commodity, a woman for sale. Although she was not royal or of noble lineage with wealthy connections, which would be the normal requisites for the demand of large ransom, she was a very valuable personage because of her achievements and notoriety. John knew that he could expect a large sum in exchange for her. He probably thought that both the Duke of Bedford, on the English side, and Charles VII, the newly-crowned king, would be rival bidders. Because he was himself the sworn vassal of the powerful Duke of Burgundy, at present an ally of the English, he would have to take that potentate's view of the matter into consideration. In the meantime, his main concern was to keep his valuable prisoner safely in custody, there being the possibility that the king or one of her former military colleagues like the Duke of Alençon, La Hire, or Dunois of Orléans, might attempt a rescue. He placed Jeanne, together with her brother and her steward, in the castle of Beaulieu which was commanded by one of his knights, Lionel de Wandomme, the man whose soldiers had actually captured her. Some days later, Duke Philip of Burgundy, with his new young wife, Isabelle of Portugal, arrived at the nearby city of Noyon. The Duchess desired to see the famous Jeanne la Pucelle, and so Jeanne was brought from the castle at Beaulieu to the bishop's palace in Noyon. John of Luxembourg and his wife were also present. This was the second time since her capture that Jeanne and the Duke had come face to face. It is not known if she had any conversation with his third wife, the young Isabelle.

Perhaps it was at that meeting, or on her return to the fortress at Beaulieu, that Jeanne heard that she was to be separated from her brother and her steward and moved to the much larger castle of Beaurevoir, nearly forty miles away, which was the fortress of John of Luxembourg himself. The news resulted in her first attempt to escape. She managed to lock her guard in the tower but was apprehended as she made her way to an outer gate. The Duke of Bedford and the University of Paris were growing impatient at the delay in handing over the woman they were already denouncing as a heretic. Another request from the University was made by the Bishop of Beauvais, Pierre Cauchon, the man who had fled from Reims at the approach of Jeanne and the French army; he was also the man the English would put in charge of her trial.

The Duke of Burgundy could have ordered his vassal, John of Luxembourg, to do a deal quickly with the English; that they both seem, on the contrary, to have slowed down the process – Jeanne was to spend four months at the castle of John of Luxembourg – is interpreted by historians as due to the influence of three noble women, all of them named Jeanne like the prisoner, who lived in the castle. They were, respectively, John's elderly aunt, his wife, and his wife's daughter by a previous marriage – her first husband was killed at Agincourt. Jeanne testified at her trial that they had all treated her kindly, offering her women's clothes or the material to make some. She also said that the elderly aunt, Jeanne of Luxembourg, 'asked my lord of Luxembourg not to deliver me to the English'. This aunt was a woman of some influence, a lady-in-waiting to the queen mother, Isabeau of Bavaria, and godmother to the new king, Charles VII. She inherited several counties and had promised to make John of Luxembourg her heir. On the other hand, John could not risk the wrath of his lord, the Duke of Burgundy, if that wily schemer decided to use Jeanne as a pawn in his intrigues with the English.

The Duke of Bedford put Bishop Pierre Cauchon in charge of the negotiations to procure the handing over of Jeanne. At this time, Cauchon was about sixty years old. He had earlier been chancellor of the University of Paris and had the reputation of being a brilliant scholar and a skilled diplomat. He had early taken the side of the university against the Pope in the disputes about the General Council, and he was a firm believer in the dual monarchy plan which he hoped would give the university more power both in secular and church affairs in France. He was also an ambitious churchman, enriching himself with many benefices and posts as was the scandalous practice of many like him. At present, he hoped that his services to the English cause would be rewarded with the archbishopric of Rouen, the captial of Normandy, which was currently vacant. The arrival of Jeanne la Pucelle on the political scene in France, and her achievement in having the Dauphin Charles crowned at Reims, had put all his schemes and ambitions in danger. The remedy was now in his own hands – that woman must be shown to be an imposter and a heretic; consequently, all her actions, including the coronation of Charles VII, would be invalid.

Bishop Cauchon met with the young King Henry VI and the

Duke of Bedford at Calais in June 1430, to discuss the bidding price for Jeanne. It was fixed at 10,000 pounds, with the addition of a pension of 300 pounds for Lionel de Wandomme, the man whose soldiers had taken her prisoner at Compiégne. The diplomatic bishop then set off on his very unspiritual mission. This sworn enemy of Jeanne la Pucelle spent the summer of 1430 in trying to arrange her sale to the English, who paid him generously for his travel and trouble. The city of Compiégne was still under siege, and Cauchon met near it with Philip of Burgundy and John of Luxembourg to convey the terms of the deal on Jeanne. They seem to have informed him of the opposition of John's aunt, the elderly and well-connected Jeanne of Luxembourg at Beaurevoir, and to have directed him to visit her while they went on with the war. The Duke of Burgundy, of course, could have simply ordered his vassal, John of Luxembourg, to hand Jeanne over to the English, but it is possible that he was prevaricating because he was weighing up all the possible consequences of the establishment of a dual monarchy of England and France, and what it might mean for his own position as the ruler of a powerful duchy within that new creation. There is no record of the discussions between the bishop and the elderly lady, Jeanne of Luxembourg, but he went away emptyhanded, to report back to the Duke of Bedford and the University of Paris merely that his mission had so far been unsuccessful. However, it is probably from that encounter that Jeanne was able to assert at her trial that Jeanne of Luxembourg did her utmost to prevent the handing over to the English of a girl whom she had personally observed now for several months and in whose goodness, purity and integrity she believed.

Cauchon's visit to the castle of John of Luxembourg had one result that might have proved disastrous to his own ambitions and to the cause of the English in France. Jeanne la Pucelle made a second attempt to escape, this time jumping from the window of a tower and injuring herself so badly that for several days she could neither eat nor drink. At her trial, she was asked why she did this – her interrogators were trying to make it into an action of despair and lack of trust in her heavenly voices. Jeanne's reply indicates that Cauchon had tried to influence the aged Jeanne of Luxembourg with visions of what would happen if Jeanne were not handed over to the Duke of Bedford. 'I had been told,' Jeanne recalled, 'that all the people in the city of Compiégne, over the age of seven years, would be slaughtered by fire and sword ... and I knew also that I was sold to the English, and I would prefer to die rather than be handed over to the English who were my enemies.'

At least Jeanne's hazardous attempt to escape is evidence that while a prisoner of John of Luxembourg she was not shackled as she would so cruelly be when she came into the power of the Duke of Bedford. She also revealed that her guiding saints told her not to believe what she had heard about the slaughter of the inhabitants of Compiégne – that city would be delivered from its besiegers 'before the feast of St Martin (November 11).' She was also reprimanded by her heavenly voices for having tried to escape. 'You will not be delivered until you have seen the king of the English, and you must accept this with a good will.' Jeanne herself did not understand whether that ambiguous *delivered* meant that she would be rescued here on earth or brought to heaven where she would be free forever from her enemies.

The obstacle to the sale of Jeanne la Pucelle was removed in September of that year, 1430, when the woman who had been protecting her, Jeanne of Luxembourg, died in Avignon where she had gone to arrange her affairs. Her nephew, John of Luxembourg, assured of his inheritance from her, was now free to close the deal with Cauchon. Both the Duke of Bedford and the University of Paris had been growing impatient with Cauchon. A letter from the university in November, before the cash had changed hands, reprimanded him: 'We note with extreme amazement that the delivery of the woman known as the Maid is now long postponed, to the prejudice of the faith and of ecclesiastical jurisdiction.' The money was paid to John of Luxembourg on 6 December, and a receipt duly issued by his squire; the wording of that receipt is worth noting: it refers to the object of sale as 'Jeanne, who is called the Maid, a prisoner of war.' John of Luxembourg knew, as everyone else did, why the English wanted to buy this woman and why they were employing Bishop Cauchon to be her judge; his conscience may have urged him to indicate that in truth she was a prisoner of war and should be treated as such and not as a heretic who, if found guilty by an ecclesiastical court, would inevitably be sentenced to death by burning at the stake.

The news that Jeanne la Pucelle, the heroine of Orléans and Reims, had been sold to the English quickly spread far and wide. While it was received with jubilation and relief in England, elsewhere it was either not believed at all or accepted with the proviso that the valiant girl who had been sent by God to deliver France from the English would herself be delivered from captivity by divine intervention. In many places in France prayers were offered for her deliverance. Her former military colleagues were powerless to do anything to help her. The king, for whom she had risked her life and shed her blood, made no effort on her behalf. After a journey lasting several weeks, Jeanne finally arrived at the city of Rouen in the English-controlled territory of Normandy, where the Duke of Bedford had decided it would be safe to put her on trial. She was lodged in the castle of Bouvreuil near the city, the official residence of Richard Beauchamp, Earl of Warwick and guardian of the young king Henry VI of England. She was to be his prisoner during the period of her trial for the next six months, chained and treated inhumanely by her warders and her judges, until her divine deliverance came when she was burnt at the stake in the marketplace of Rouen on 30 May 1431.

CHAPTER TEN

Trial by Theologians

The trial of Jeanne la Pucelle lasted for five months, from 9 January to 30 May 1431. From beginning to end it was not only unfair but illegal, the object of the proceedings being not to decide on valid evidence whether the defendant should be adjudged innocent or guilty, but to ensure that Jeanne be found unequivocally guilty of heresy, with the inevitable consequence that she would be sentenced to death by burning. Also, although the trial was conducted by an ecclesiastical tribunal and allegedly according to the procedures of the Inquisition set up by the church for such heresy trials, it was really a political trial, organised, paid for, and vicariously controlled by the Duke of Bedford and his uncle, Cardinal Beaufort of Westminster, to further their plan of uniting France with England under the new king, Henry VI. In order to achieve this objective, it was essential that the newly-crowned King of France, Charles VII, be dethroned and disqualified. The condemnation for heresy of Jeanne la Pucelle, the woman who had claimed to be sent by God to have Charles crowned, would be sufficient to discredit his legitimacy in the eyes of the church and of all the royal houses of Europe.

Having been put in charge, by the Duke of Bedford, of the negotiations for the purchase of Jeanne from the Burgundians, Pierre Cauchon, Bishop of Beauvais, with the aid of his erstwhile colleagues at the University of Paris, had then worked himself into the position of head of the tribunal set up to conduct this crucial trial. He was now faced with the problem of giving his English employers value for their money with a showpiece ecclesiastical trial that, while seeming legal and fair, not only to Rome, but to all of Europe, would result in the pre-arranged verdict. As an experienced negotiator and professional theologian himself, and with a tribunal consisting of almost fifty theologians and lawyers from various religious orders and universities, Cauchon must have felt that the trial of this illiterate peasant girl would proceed swiftly and smoothly to its envisaged result. While he was being well paid by Bedford for his services, he must have hoped also that his prominence in this spectacular affair would enhance his own reputation and result in advancement both in the church and in the European political arena.

According to the rules of the Inquisition, a trial for heresy should be conducted by the bishop of the diocese where the offence occurred or by the bishop of the native diocese of the person accused. However, the French now controlled Beauvais, and so Pierre Cauchon was a fugitive from his own diocese; but since the Duke of Bedford wanted the trial to take place at Rouen in Normandy, strongly held by the English, this should have disqualified Cauchon from presiding. That legal obstacle was removed by the church authorities in Rouen. At the request of the Duke of Bedford, they granted Cauchon what was described as 'a commission of territory', allowing him to preside at Rouen.

A further violation of the rules of the Inquisition, to which Jeanne herself adverted as soon as the trial began, was that she should have been held in a women's prison and guarded by women, whereas she was held for the duration of the trial in the castle of the Earl of Warwick and guarded by uncouth and foul-mouthed English soldiers. With the connivance of Cardinal Beaufort, Cauchon circumvented this blatant injustice by having three keys made for the lock on Jeanne's cell, one to be held by the Cardinal, another by Cauchon himself, and the third by the vice-inquisitor, a theologian who would be appointed by the head of the Inquisition in France; all three being clergymen, Jeanne was officially stated to be 'in ecclesiastical custody'. Her protests at not being in a women's prison and guarded by women were ignored; possibly, they were countered by the spurious argument that her insistence on wearing men's clothes entitled her judges to treat her as a male prisoner.

Even before the trial opened on 9 January 1431, Cauchon had taken two preliminary actions that, if productive, would have made the trial more of a matter of form, perhaps even unnecessary. The first was based on what may be called the defendant's chosen *nom de guerre, viz* Jeanne la Pucelle. Even if his intelligence sources had informed him of the examination for virginity to which Jeanne had been subjected at Poitiers two years earlier, when the Dauphin Charles was still undecided about her, he now ordered another such examination, hoping, perhaps, that Jeanne's involvement in military campaigns since then might have negated her claim to that title and so enable him to proclaim her immoral and a liar even before the trial began. He was to suffer his first disappointment and setback. The examination, conducted by chosen matrons under the direction of Anne of Burgundy, wife of the Duke of Bedford himself, resulted in the same positive result as the previous test, vindicating yet again the morality and purity of Jeanne la Pucelle.

The other step taken by Cauchon was to send a commission of inquiry to Domrémy to collect evidence about Jeanne's behaviour that might prove prejudicial to her. Having spent several weeks interviewing people and priests in her own village and in several neighbouring villages, the chief of the commission made a report to Cauchon, summing up their findings with a personal comment that seems to indicate how he himself now regarded the whole affair: 'I found nothing about Jeanne la Pucelle that I would not wish to find about my own sister.' It must have caused Cauchon to gnash his teeth and regret that he had tried that particular avenue of investigation.

Between Cauchon and the Earl of Warwick, in whose castle the trial was to be held, the conditions of confinement devised for Jeanne were so harsh that in modern times they would be regarded as cruelty to an animal. Initially, perhaps to strengthen the common English belief that Jeanne was a witch who might fly away at any moment, Cauchon caused an iron cage to be made in which the prisoner could be kept standing upright, chained by the neck, hands and feet. Someone, perhaps the

Duke of Bedford or the Duchess of Burgundy, must have caused him to opt for the lesser method used all through her trial – day and night she wore irons on her legs, while at night the chain on these was attached to another chain at the foot of her bed and linked to a heavy block of wood about six feet long. A royal squire, John Grey, with two other Englishmen assisting him, was put in charge of the prisoner; all three had to swear on the Bible that nobody would be allowed access to the prisoner except with the personal authorisation of Cauchon. They set five English soldiers to guard her, three of whom slept in her cell at night, the other two outside the door. What Jeanne endured by way of obscene insult and mockery from these soldiers, described as 'of the lowest kind', can be imagined; she complained several times, to Cauchon and others, that one or other of them had tried to violate her, and she repeatedly asked to be transferred to a women's prison, all to no avail. With regard to her diet or her personal needs, nothing is on record except that on one occasion she became unwell after eating some fish – it was probably just badly cooked, since neither Bedford nor Cauchon wanted their precious victim to die otherwise than tied to a stake in the public square of Rouen.

As in many castles like that of the Earl of Warwick near Rouen, the cell in which a prisoner might be confined was in a position where a person in an adjacent passage or tunnel, or in a room above, could overhear conversations. Bishop Cauchon added an even more devious and scandalous method of gleaning evidence: he arranged for a priest, Nicholas Loiseleur, to visit Jeanne several times, pretending to be a prisoner himself and from her native province. After he had won her confidence, Loiseleur kindly offered to hear her confession. He did so, and later in the trial it was revealed that several persons were posted in the corner near her cell where it was possible to overhear her confession; like the commission at Domrémy, they garnered nothing that Cauchon could use against her.

The rules of the Inquisition required that two judges preside at a trial for heresy, one of them being the inquisitor for the diocese. Cauchon invited that official, a Dominican friar named Jean Lemaître, resident in Rouen, to fulfil that function. Friar Lemaître, however, at first refused the offer, observing that his conscience would not allow him to become involved since his jurisdiction applied only to the diocese of Rouen – a clear indication that others like him must have been aware of the illegality of the affair. In fact, the Bishop of Avranches wrote a letter formally opposing the trial – this protest was, of course, omitted from the records of the trial – and several other clerics in Rouen itself, especially some of the Dominican theologians, expressed concern or total opposition, one of the latter being summarily imprisoned for his protests. In order to ensure that the trial would be formally an affair of the church and the Inquisition, Cauchon applied to the higher authority of the Grand Inquisitor of France, who ordered Friar Lemaître to accept the bishop's offer to lend the prestige of his office to the proceedings. He did so, albeit with some delay, and absented himself often, which did not trouble Cauchon who preferred to preside alone. The man who was to be the official prosecutor, Jean d'Estivet, was closely connected with Cauchon, being a canon of Cauchon's own episcopal cathedral at Beauvais. As will be seen later, he was one of the most antagonistic interrogators of Jeanne, and several witnesses later testified that whenever he visited her in her cell he insulted her in lewd and vulgar terms as if she were a common prostitute. He was also responsible for the drastically altered version of the transcript of the trial that was sent all over Europe by Cauchon and the Duke of Bedford. That Jeanne stood alone, and in shackles, without a lawyer to defend her, all through the five months of the trial, was another feature that was not in accord with the procedure laid down for such trials.

For its drama, and for the fact that its procedures were only a legalistic camouflage for the preconceived verdict, the trial of Jeanne d'Arc at Rouen in 1431 ranks with the trial of St Thomas More for treason at London in 1535, and the trial of Our Lord Jesus Christ himself for blasphemy at Jerusalem some time in the third decade of the Christian era; but in its length and documentation, Jeanne's trial outdoes those other notorious historic charades; indeed, it must be one of the most meticulously documented trials ever to take place. The records of all such trials by the Inquisition had to be preserved in the ecclesiastical archives, but Cauchon may have also wanted to be able to produce evidence from the records to justify the verdict in years to come. He assigned three professional notaries to record the proceedings which were in French, although later to be translated into Latin for the church archives. As the trial proceeded, and Jeanne's replies to some of the theologians' questions began to be an embarrassment for Cauchon personally and a cause of concern for the learned members of the tribunal, he ordered that her replies be recorded in indirect speech rather than verbatim. The full transcipt of the condemnation trial is extant in three authenticated manuscripts.

At the very first session of the trial, Cauchon tried to make Jeanne promise that she would not try to escape, 'under penalty of being convicted of heresy' – considering how she was chained and manacled, and guarded day and night by five soldiers, she would have needed to be the mythical Hercules in order even to attempt it. His farcical prohibition was thrown back in his face when Jeanne said, 'I do not accept that condition; if I did escape, how could that cause me to be blamed for having offended against my faith?' He then tried to get her to swear an oath. Jeanne again refused because, she said, she did not know what they were going to ask her, and there were some things that had been revealed to her and that she would never tell them 'even if you cut my head off'. Cauchon then suddenly ordered her, in a ploy that was not in accordance with the rules, to recite the Lord's Prayer, the *Pater Noster*. For the third time, he was rebuffed. 'I will recite that prayer for you,' Jeanne said, 'if you will hear my confession.' Any member of the tribunal who was not biased against her must have felt like clapping: at one stroke, she had reminded this French bishop, acting on behalf of his English masters, that he was a priest, and she had challenged him to function in his sacerdotal role in the confessional, where he would be able to learn the exact nature of her belief in God and in the teaching of the Catholic Church. Cauchon did not accept that challenge.

During all the ensuing sessions of the trial, in spite of the inexorable physical and mental effect of the brutal conditions of her confinement, Jeanne put up a spirited resistance to all the efforts of the tribunal's theologians and lawyers to make her admit to anything that could be used against her. Indeed, her replies to those learned doctors lead one inevitably to recall the words of Jesus to his disciples when he foretold that his followers would be reviled and persecuted: 'When you are brought before their councils and judges, do not trouble about how you shall answer; the Holy Spirit will tell you what to answer.' The ambitious politician in Cauchon must have been far stronger as an influence than any sacerdotal piety; even from the outset of the trial, it was evident that this illiterate peasant girl was either a naturally skilled casuist or a truly devout soul guided by the grace of God. One of the most famous of her replies concerned that very point. When she said, in the course of one bout of interrogation, 'If it were not for the grace of God, I would not know how to do anything,' one of the judges immediately spotted the opportunity to ask a question that was as clever as those problems concocted by the Pharisees or the Sadducees to pose to Jesus in order, as the evangelist says, 'to entrap him'. Question and answer deserve to be recorded here exactly as they were noted down on the day when they were spoken:

'Savez-vous si vous êtes en la grâce de Dieu?'
'Si je n'y suis, Dieu m'y mette, et si j'y suis, Dieu m'y garde.'
('Do you know that you are in the grace of God?'
'If I am not, may God put me there, and if I am, may God keep me there').

The notary who wrote down those words attested later to the effect of that inspired response: 'Those who were interrogating her were all astonished.' So were theologians all over Europe when the record of that trial became widely known; so famous did Jeanne's reply become that it was formed into a popular prayer.

CHAPTER ELEVEN

A Question of Clothes

The trial was divided into a preliminary period for the collection of the evidence and the formulation of charges, with the second period forming the trial proper. To Jeanne, dragging her shackled legs wearily along every time the usher, Jean Massieu, brought her from her cell to face the tribunal, those formal divisions meant little. The method varied little, the intensity, casuistry, and sometimes the banality, of the questions put to her causing her sometimes to protest that she did not understand, or even to ask her learned interrogators to please speak one by one. She ridiculed some of the more banal queries, such as, 'Did the saints have hair?' 'Now, that's an important point!' 'Did St Michael wear clothes?' 'Do you think God can't afford to dress his saints?' 'Did St Margaret speak English?' 'Why should she speak English – she is not of the English party!' In effect, the theologians and lawyers were going over the same ground as their counterparts who had examined Jeanne for three weeks at Poitiers – she sometimes even referred them to that examination, the result of which was a solemn ecclesiastical declaration that she was entirely free from any taint of unorthodoxy in her Christian faith. Yet, for five months these repetitive interrogations went on – about her heavenly voices and the saints she named as having spoken to her, about her wearing men's clothes, about her youth and her beliefs, about any and every aspect of her life and career – and produced not a whit of evidence that could be used to bring a charge of heresy against her. In fact, no such formal charge was ever made, which was another blatant breach of the church's own regulations.

There was nothing contrary to the teaching of the church in

Jeanne's claim that saints or angels had been sent to her with divine instructions about her life and course of action, nor in her freely-offered assertion, during one session, that angels come on earth much more often than people think; that was a statement with which the learned theologians could hardly disagree in view of the church's teaching with regard to our personal guardian angel and the many instances of angelic visitation in the scriptures, including that seismic visit of the Angel Gabriel to 'a virgin whose name was Mary' in a village in Palestine. They would also have been familiar with St Augustine's *City of God*, written a thousand years earlier and regarded ever since as one of the greatest books ever written. The great bishop of Hippo would be in total agreement with the peasant girl from Domrémy, and any reader of his book, even in its necessarily abridged version – it is really twenty-two books in one – will come away with a strongly enhanced feeling of the existence of spirits both good and evil.

When Jeanne was asked if she were loyal to the Pope, she turned the question to her advantage by appealing to have her case heard by the Pope, in order to prove that she was loyal to the teachings and doctrine of the Catholic Church; her appeal was ignored. When Cauchon brought up the matter of the threatening letter she had dictated to the King of England and his agents in France before she even arrived at Orléans, Jeanne again astonished the members of the tribunal and angered some, including the Cardinal Beaufort, by not only admitting that she was the author of that letter but by predicting that 'before seven years are over, the English will suffer even more terrible losses than they did at Orléans, and they will be driven out of France altogether.' This was not the kind of report the Duke of Bedford wanted to hear coming from any session of the tribunal.

Jeanne herself revealed that her heavenly voices were preparing her for what was to be the outcome of the farcical trial. 'St Catherine told me that I would have help, but I do not know if this will be my deliverance from captivity or my deliverance when I face judgement. My voices say: "Take everything

THE ONE WHO LED AN ARMY

serenely, do not shrink from your martyrdom; from that you will finally come to the kingdom of paradise." I call this a martyrdom because of what I suffer in this imprisonment. I do not know if I will have to suffer more, but I defer in this as in everything to the will of our Lord.'

Although, when they questioned her about wearing men's clothes, Jeanne had replied that she did this only because she had been directed to do so by her voices, Cauchon and his accomplices began increasingly to see in this abnormal behaviour the basis for a charge that could be used for their purpose. Perhaps warned by her heavenly counsellors, Jeanne herself must have realised that Cauchon would eventually settle on this as evidence that she was not willing to obey the church. Whatever the reason, she surely caused some emotion among the more pious and fair-minded of her fifty or so interrogators and judges at one session when, as the topic was brought up yet again, she suddenly ignored the tribunal altogether and began to pray aloud. Her prayer concerned this aspect of her career to which so much importance was now being attached. Even the notary, the copyists, and the translators, must have been impressed by this sudden and sincere expression of piety and trust in God: it was left in the records exactly as she uttered it, without being altered into indirect speech or translated into Latin:

Très doux Dieu, en l'honneur de votre Sainte Passion, je vous requiers, si vous m'aimez, que vous me révéliez comment je dois répondre à ces gens d'Église. Je sais bien, quant a l'habit, le commandement comment je l'ai pris; mais je ne sais point par quelle manière je dois laisser. Pour ce, plaise vous à moi l'enseigner.

(Most gracious God, in honour of your sacred passion, I beg of you, as you love me, that you let me know how to reply to these people of the church. With regard to the clothes, I know well how I received the command; but I do not know in what way I ought to finish with it. For this, that it may please you to direct me.)

When Cauchon saw that he was making very little profit

from the interrogations before the whole tribunal, and that even some members were beginning to voice discordant opinions, he resorted to other tactics. With one or two others, he began to conduct interrogations in Jeanne's cell, going over the same ground and receiving the same answers. On the occasion when Jeanne became ill after eating fish, she was visited by several doctors, one of them being the personal physician of the Duchess of Bedford, another sent by the English Cardinal Beaufort and the Earl of Warwick, owner of the castle; such care was not for love of the unfortunate prisoner, as was explained in later testimony by the doctor summoned by Beaufort and Warwick: 'The Earl ordered us to take care of her, because more than anything in the world the king did not wish her to die a natural death. He had bought her dearly and considered her very precious, and he did not wish her to die except at the hands of justice, and that she should be burned.' He and other doctors also testified that they were brought to Jeanne's cell by Jean d'Estivet, the canon of Beauvais who was prosecutor of the trial, and that this cleric called Jeanne 'a slut and a whore, offering her many other insults'.

When Cauchon finally decided to end the interrogations, it was this same Jean d'Estivet who was put in charge of drawing up a brief in the form of seventy articles based on the voluminous transcripts of the five-month trial. In these articles, he expanded on most of the questions that had been put to her, while distorting and falsifying, sometimes with lewd and vulgar connotations, many of her answers. This brief had to be read aloud to Jeanne. She protested vigorously at the untruths and distortions, some of them, like the accusation that she had often used charms to work magic, so blatantly contrary to what she had told the tribunal that the very notaries who had written down her replies later condemned the comprehensive falsification carried out by the unscrupulous d'Estivet, obviously under the direction of his bishop, Pierre Cauchon. One significant article referred to Jeanne's male clothes, describing them as very shortened and dissolute. Jeanne's angry retort to this was included in the French transcript but omitted in the Latin version prepared later for dissemination in France and abroad.

The final article of the seventy was crucial; it referred to a topic on which she had been questioned at length during the trial, whether she was willing to submit to the church militant (even some members of the tribunal had suggested in vain that such technical terminology should be explained to the prisoner). Jeanne's reply as given in the transcript is worth study: 'I am willing to obey the church so long as she does not command me something that is impossible, and by impossible I mean that I should revoke the actions I have done and the things I have said in this trial about the visions and revelations that were given to me from God. These I will not revoke for anyone. If the church should order that I do something against the commandment that was given me by God, I would not do it for anything.'

Jeanne, enlightened by the Holy Spirit, is here stating succinctly what theologians had been discussing at length for centuries, the supreme authority of conscience in religious and moral matters. After Luther's revolt in 1517, the question would become even more contentious, and there are still many Protestants who believe that Catholics cannot obey their conscience because they must obey the Pope whom they believe to be infallible. The English politician, Gladstone, made this assertion in 1874, after the doctrine of infallibility had been promulgated at the Vatican Council of 1870. In an essay entitled, *The Vatican Decrees and their Bearing on Civil Allegiance*, he declared that the doctrine meant that a Catholic could not be loyal to the state *and* to the Pope as head of the church. He was answered comprehensively by John Henry Newman, the most brilliant intellectual of the century, a convert who knew both the Catholic and Protestant views, having been reared a bigoted Protestant who believed firmly, at the age of fifteen, that the Pope was anti-Christ.

Quoting St Thomas Aquinas and other authorities, Newman also directed Gladstone's attention to the decree of a previous council of the church, the fourth Lateran Council in 1215, which declared: *'Quidquid fit contra conscientiam, aedificat ad gehennam:* Whatever is done contrary to one's conscience leads to eternal damnation.' In passing, Newman also adverted to the modern misuse of the term conscience when disconnected from belief in God, the divine authority of which conscience is the voice: 'When men (now) advocate the rights of conscience, they in no sense mean the rights of the Creator, nor the duty to him, in thought and deed, of the creature; but the right of thinking, speaking, writing, and acting according to their judgement or their humour, without any thought of God at all ... Conscience is a stern monitor, but in this century it has been superseded by a counterfeit which the eighteen centuries prior to it never heard of, and could not have mistaken for it if they had. It is the right of self-will.'

Whatever some of the theologians in the tribunal may have thought of Jeanne's distinction between a message from God and an order from the church – two of them, including Friar Isambart de la Pierre from the Dominican convent in Rouen, incurred the wrath of Cauchon by advising Jeanne on the question and its dangers for her – Cauchon interpreted it as a refusal to submit to the authority of the church militant. The only evidence of such refusal was in the matter of her male clothes, a topic on which, as she herself pointed out repeatedly, she had already been examined and cleared by the church tribunal at Poitiers two years before.

CHAPTER TWELVE

Deliverence

The procedural rules now laid down that the seventy articles be condensed into twelve, these to be submitted to theologians and ecclesiastical lawyers who had not been directly involved in the trial. The anti-papal doctors of the University of Paris approved the articles at once, as did many other ecclesiastics, including the Bishops of Lisieux and Coutances, all of them listed in the payment accounts of the King of England. Others, however, raised various objections; these included three abbots, eleven church lawyers in Rouen itself, and individual theologians, some of the latter demanding that the whole question should be submitted to the Pope, as Jeanne herself had repeatedly requested.

Ignoring all dissenting opinion from such sources, and the fact that the long trial with its innumerable sessions of interrogation had produced no verdict and no charge, Cauchon went ahead with the job for which his increasingly impatient English masters were paying him. The ritual of the Inquisition required that a heretic be given 'charitable warnings' in the hope that they would recant. Cauchon conducted these on 18 April and 2 May, again submitting Jeanne to questions about obedience to the church. Jeanne was now weak and unwell, as she herself told him, but she repeated her defence: 'I am a good Christian, and well baptised, and I shall die a good Christian ... I believe fully in the church here on earth, and that it cannot fail or err; but with regard to what I have done and said, I rely on God, who has told me to do what I have done.'

A week later, Jeanne was again brought from her cell by the usher, Jean Massieu. He led her, shackled as always, into the great tower of the castle. Waiting for her were Cauchon himself with some other assessors of the tribunal, but also confronting the prisoner were two laymen whom she had never seen before. They were the executioner, Leparmentier, and his assistant. Cauchon threatened her with torture if she did not alter her statements and her attitude. Jeanne gave him the logical answer to any use of torture in any age for the purpose of making prisoners talk: 'You can pull all my body apart if you wish until my soul leaves my body, but I will not tell you anything else – and if I did tell you something, afterwards I shall say that it was only because you made me say it by torture.' Cauchon had no qualms about the use of torture – it was commonly used in state trials all over Europe, and for centuries afterwards – but when he put it to an assembly of the assessors, only a small minority approved, the others dissenting for the very reason given by Jeanne herself.

An event occurred on the following day, Sunday 13 May 1431, which is not recorded in the official transcripts of the trial. It was a banquet given in the castle by Richard Beauchamp, Earl of Warwick, at which many of the guests were people who had been involved in the career of the young woman who, while they were feasting – the Earl's account book gives a long list of the food and drink purchased for the banquet – was confined, chained, ill and apprehensive, in a cell where her vulgar guards were probably taunting her with her approaching death at the stake. What is truly bizarre about this episode is that, having wined and dined, Warwick and his guests went to that cell to see and speak to Jeanne. Although Cauchon and the Bishop of Noyon, Jean de Mailly, were guests at the dinner, they did not join the others in that cruel post-prandial entertainment, for such it truly was; neither, apparently, did any of the noble ladies. Among those whom Jeanne saw enter her cell were John of Luxembourg, the man who had sold her to the English, and his brother, Louis, who was the Bishop of Thérouanne, and the Earl of Stafford.

A Burgundian noble, Aimond de Macy, who had previously met Jeanne at the castle of Beaurevoir where she was first imprisoned, gave an account of that ignoble encounter. John of

Luxembourg told Jeanne that he had come to Rouen to pay a ransom for her, on condition that she would never again take up arms against them. To which the prisoner replied, 'In God's name, I know that you are mocking me, because I know well that you have neither the power nor the will to do that.' When he repeated the assertion, Jeanne said, 'I know it is certain that the English want me put to death, because they think they will then have the whole kingdom of France; but even if there were a hundred thousand more of them, they will never have France.' At which prophetic words, the Earl of Stafford was so angry that he began to pull his dagger from its scabbard to strike her, but Warwick prevented him.

On that day, Warwick informed Cauchon that the English authorities wanted the business brought to an end quickly. Soon after, the University of Paris sent him a letter to the same effect. It was time, they said, to put an end to the 'scandalous demoralisation of the faithful, caused by a woman named Jeanne who is called the Maid.' Lest anyone be in doubt about the guilt of the said Jeanne, the professors at Paris, commenting on the twelve articles sent them by Cauchon, categorically declared this woman, whom they had never met or questioned, to be an apostate, a heretic, a liar and a schismatic.

On Thursday 24 May, Jeanne was subjected to another strange ordeal. Several platforms were erected in a public cemetery. To one of these, Jeanne was led by her usher, Jean Massieu, the others being occupied by many bishops and dignitaries, under the presidency of Cardinal Beaufort of Westminster. A canon of Rouen, Guillaume Érard, then proceeded to preach a formal sermon at Jeanne, the content of which was an accusation that she had consistently refused to submit to the church. Jeanne countered this with her usual defence, again appealing that her case be heard by the Pope. The preacher repeated his assertions three times. A formal piece of parchment, known as a *cedula* (from Latin, meaning to concede or give up) was then presented to Jeanne by an English official, Laurence Calot, secretary of the King of England, who ordered her to sign it. The usher, Jean

Massieu, who read it to Jeanne, and other witnesses who saw it, testified many years later that this document contained about eight lines of writing. When the altered and falsified transcript of Jeanne's trial was eventually circulated, the *cedula* she signed that day had grown from about eight lines – it was only the length of a *Pater Noster*, according to one witness – to forty-seven in the French version and forty-four in Latin, containing a much amplified declaration of recantation from many of the aberrations of which Jeanne had been falsely accused during her trial.

The actual content of the document offered to Jeanne was an abjuration of her heretical views and a promise not to wear men's clothes in future. The notary who had been in charge of the recording of her trial, Guillaume Manchon, testified later that Jeanne laughed when presented with it, although the usher, Jean Massieu, said that he thought Jeanne did not understand it. He said she demanded that the document should be examined by the priests and that they should advise her about it. This request met only with an order from the priest who had preached at her: 'Do it now or you will end your life by fire.' Laurence Calot then held her hand and forced her to sign it. Jeanne did not sign the document with her name, as she had signed some letters, but with a circle. Calot then forced her to add a cross.

Apparently it was not unusual to add a *cedula*, containing some relevant material, to a legal document. Its use in the context of the condemnation of Jeanne seems to have been an elaborate trick on the part of Cauchon to trap her – perhaps she did laugh sarcastically when she realised this. However, his English masters must not have been aware of what was in his scheming mind, because when the *cedula* was produced, and signed with a mark by Jeanne, there was consternation among the English potentates on the other platforms. If, as seemed apparent, Jeanne had signed, albeit by force, a recantation of her alleged heretical views, the effect would be to substitute some years in a church prison for death at the stake. The Earl of Warwick took Cauchon to task, angrily informing him that the king's money had been wasted because Jeanne would now escape death; but Cauchon re-assured him, telling him that they would still catch her.

He took the first step in that process when Jeanne asked that she be taken now to a church prison and not left in the hands of the English; this was her right if she had signed a document promising to obey the church, but Cauchon's response was to order her to be taken back to the same cell from which she had been brought. This contravened both the church law and all the promises Jeanne had been given during her trial, but it was to prove the master stroke in Cauchon's plan.

Three days after the sermon in the cemetery, it was reported to Cauchon that Jeanne had reverted to wearing men's clothes. One of the Dominican friars who attended Jeanne in her last hours testified that she told him she did this because an English lord had entered her cell and tried to violate her; but her usher, Jean Massieu, said that, when she woke up on the morning of Trinity Sunday, she could not find her women's clothes because her English guards had taken them away and gave her only a bag full of men's clothes in which she had no option but to dress. This latter version would fit in with the scheme of Cauchon, but perhaps Jeanne was put under pressure in several ways in order to force her decision quickly. However it was brought about, her decision was legal evidence that she had contravened her signed recantation and meant that she could now be officially sentenced as a relapsed heretic, again disobeying the church.

Together with the official vice-inquisitor, Jean Lemaître, and other members of the tribunal, Cauchon came to Jeanne's cell next morning. She was formally questioned about her reasons for resuming men's clothes, and answered that the promises made to her had not been kept. She was asked if her voices had spoken to her about the matter, and she replied, 'God has expressed, through St Margaret and St Catherine, his great sorrow at the strong treason to which I agreed in abjuring and making a revocation to save my life, and said that I was damning myself to save my life.' She added, however, that she had not intended to deny her voices or her apparitions. When Cauchon left her, he conveyed the good news to the Earl of Warwick and others who were waiting outside. 'You can be cheerful now,' he said, 'it is done.'

Early in the morning on Wednesday 30 May, two Dominican friars came to Jeanne's cell to prepare her for death. One of them later gave an account of that scene. Jeanne was humanly distressed at the thought of how she was to die. She wept bitterly and tore her hair, crying, 'I would prefer to be beheaded many times than to be burned!' Friar Martin Ladvenu, who had been among the assessors at her trial, heard her confession. She complained of how she had been treated by her jailers and others while in that prison for five months. Later, Bishop Cauchon himself arrived and Jeanne greeted him with a direct accusation: 'Bishop, it is because of you that I am to die.' He countered by saying that she had not kept her promise and had returned to what he called her 'first witchcraft'. But Jeanne again accused him of not having treated her according to the rules of the church itself. If he had done so, this would not have happened to her. 'And that is why,' she said, 'I complain of you to God.'

After Cauchon had left, Jeanne asked the friars to give her Holy Communion. This caused a problem for them – according to the laws of the church, a heretic was excommunicate, and therefore could not receive the sacraments. One of them had already heard Jeanne's confession, but to take the further step of giving her Holy Communion might have involved them in deeper trouble. They sent the usher, Jean Massieu, to Cauchon with their problem. His response was in itself a contravention of the church's laws: 'Tell them to give her the Eucharist, and anything else she asks.' It reveals, perhaps, the sacerdotal conscience still lingering beneath the surface of the diplomatic prelate's ambitions. That evening, Jeanne was again brought from her cell to be subjected to a final sermon about her errors, this time in the marketplace of Rouen where platforms had been set up like those in the cemetery on the preceding day.

Next day, the English Cardinal Beaufort presided at an assembly of forty-two of the assessors who had taken part in the trial of Jeanne. He informed them of Jeanne's blatant breach of her promise to obey the instruction of the church and asked for their opinions as to what should now be done with her. The Cardinal and Cauchon must have been taken aback to find that only three of the assessors favoured handing Jeanne over to the secular power; the other thirty-nine recommended that the crucial *cedula* be read over to her again and properly explained. It is often forgotten, or ignored, by historians hostile to religion, that in Europe at that time, when politics and religion were so intertwined, the state regarded heresy as a crime just as dangerous as treason, since those who were subversive in religion were often just as revolutionary in matters of state; also, that although the state considered a church court the appropriate place to try people charged with heresy, it reserved the right to sentence and execute anyone found guilty by the theologians and inquisitors. The Romans imposed a similar restriction on their subject nations, although the Catholic theologians of the Inquisition were more assured of having the death sentence rubber-stamped by the state officials than were the Jewish theologians of the Sanhedrin when they brought Jesus before the obstreperous Roman governor, Pontius Pilate, after a hurried midnight trial, as illegal as the long-drawn-out one that convicted Jeanne la Pucelle, had achieved the desired result.

Those dissenting assessors, although in such an overwhelming majority, had nothing more than a consultative voice in the matter. Cauchon and his English masters were resolved to waste no more time. Indeed, they were in such haste to achieve their final objective that Cauchon and the Cardinal again flouted the rules of the Inquisition and the church. Having found Jeanne guilty, they should then have handed her over to the bailiffs of Rouen to be formally sentenced to death and executed. The bailiffs themselves testified later that they were ignored. Jeanne was brought straight from her cell to the stake in the marketplace, where all was in readiness, on the morning of Wednesday 30 May 1431. Her usher, Jean Massieu, was present, as were, he said, many hundreds of armed soldiers ensuring that the populace were kept well back. All those who gave testimony later agreed on how she died, crying out the holy name, Jesus, many times. When she was being tied to the stake, she asked to have a cross, and an English soldier quickly made a little cross from some of the wood that was piled in bundles around her. This she kissed and then placed in her bosom. Friar Isambart, one of the two Rouen Dominicans who had attended her in her cell and was still trying to minister to her, ran to a nearby church and brought back a processional crucifix which he held high as the flames rose about her, 'so that,' he said, 'the cross on which Our Saviour hung could be continually before her eyes.' The executioner who had been called in to frighten her in the prison, Leparmantier, recalled: 'Once the fire rose around her, she cried out many times, Jesus!, and especially in her last breath, she cried out with a great cry, Jesus!, so that all present heard it and many wept with pity.' Even some of her enemies, including the Bishop of Thérouanne, Louis of Luxembourg, and some of those who had been assessors at her trial were seen to weep, one canon saying to the people near him, 'I wish that my soul were where I believe this woman's soul is today.'

Public executions, by burning or other gruesome methods, were common all over Europe, but Jeanne's youth and innocence – of which many even among those who had assisted at her trial seemed now convinced – and especially the extraordinary manner in which she met her death, made a profound impression on the onlookers. Friar Isambart recorded that even the executioner was troubled; he came to the Dominican convent in Rouen later that day, apparently seeking confession, and told the friars he felt he was damned because he had burned a holy woman.

Cauchon and the Earl of Warwick were concerned only that there should be no repercussions arising from so-called relics of that same woman. Warwick ordered her remains to be collected and thrown into the Seine. Rumour and pious wishful thinking soon began to create stories that Jeanne's heart did not burn in spite of post-mortem attempts by the executioner using sulphur, or even that the woman who died was not really Jeanne la Pucelle. Many people throughout France had believed either that King Charles VII would rescue Jeanne, or that God would deliver her from prison and death by a miracle. As far as Cauchon and the English were concerned, however, Jeanne la Pucelle was burned to ashes, and so, in Cauchon's own words, the job was done.

CHAPTER THIRTEEN

Rising from the Ashes

The news of the death of Jeanne la Pucelle, while causing sadness to the French, as well as disappointment and anger that she had not been ransomed or rescued, was a cause of jubilation and relief for the English, inspiring them to a renewal of their military action. The spectacular success of Jeanne's military campaign was widely believed by the common English soldiers to be due to her being a witch aided by the powers of evil – we have seen the Duke of Bedford's problems in enlisting fresh troops in England because of this belief.

It is difficult nowadays to appreciate the effect of such beliefs and superstitions in former ages, but it will surprise the modern reader to learn that the Stuart who was King James VI of Scotland, and became also King James I of England in 1603, wrote a book entitled *Daemonology* against witchcraft – he toned down his attitude later – and that in England alone, seventy thousand women were executed for that crime between 1600 and 1680. Even Anne Boleyn, the mother of Queen Elizabeth, was accused of being a witch and was sentenced 'to be beheaded or burned at the king's pleasure'. Belief in witches and other sources of evil was not confined to the common people. When he was annoyed by flies while writing, Luther, in Manichean mood, accused Satan of having created flies purposely to distract people like him when writing good books. When Calvin's version of religious reform took control in Geneva, people were burned at the stake having been accused of crimes such as contaminating others with the plague. It is not surprising, then, that the elimination of the woman they believed to be a witch and invincible should have injected new confidence into the English troops and their leaders.

The Duke of Bedford and the Earl of Warwick renewed their campaign in France in the weeks after Jeanne's death, and by the end of the year the French troops must have been regretting even more that Jeanne la Pucelle was not leading them into battle with her sacred standard waving them on. The militant Archbishop of Reims, Regnault of Chartres, who had at first sided with Jeanne and later turned against her, produced his protégé, the shepherd boy he claimed would do just as much as La Pucelle, at one of the battles, with the result that the French were again routed and the poor lad taken prisoner along with many knights and soldiers. The English mocked the event with the name, 'Battle of the Shepherd', and did not even consider demanding a ransom for him. In December 1431, six months after Jeanne's death, when the nine-year-old Henry VI of England was crowned King of France in Paris, the shepherd boy was paraded through the city as part of the procession; subsequently, he was sewn into a leather sack and thrown into the Seine. The coronation itself, intended to establish Henry's claim to the dual monarchy, would soon prove to have been a futile display of pomp and circumstance.

While his English employers, embarking on their new military campaign, were confident that they would now reap the benefit of the vast sums they had spent on discrediting King Charles VII through the trial of Jeanne – and the ransom of 10,000 pounds was only a portion of their overall expenditure – Bishop Pierre Cauchon was already concerned that the trial and execution of Jeanne la Pucelle could have negative repercussions in the political as well as in the ecclesiastical affairs in which his personal ambitions were centred. Already, on the day before her execution, he had been given a clear intimation of possible future trouble when only three of the forty-two assessors of the trial had supported his view that Jeanne was a relapsed heretic and should be sentenced to death without further ado. He must have realised also that some of those involved in the trial had become increasingly dubious about the whole affair, while others later admitted that they had been afraid to voice their objections through fear of incurring the wrath of Cauchon and his English masters.

That such fears were well founded is seen in Cauchon's treatment of the first person to instigate a formal protest about the trial. This was Friar Pierre Bosquier, a member of the Dominican community at the convent of Saint-Jacques in Rouen, and a colleague of Friar Isambart de La Pierre, who had raised the crucifix for the dying Jeanne to see, and of Friar Martin Ladvenu who had been an assessor in the trial and had also heard Jeanne's last confession and given her the Viaticum. Cauchon silenced the outspoken Friar Bosquier by summarily sentencing him to a year in prison on bread and water, probably for publicly questioning the verdict of a church trial. He then convened a meeting of some of the trial assessors of whose loyalty and obedience he was sure, and got them to agree with him in a declaration that Jeanne had formally denied her voices and revelations, confessing that she had come to realise that they were evil, and that she regretted all the harm she had done because of them. Significantly, however, and much to Cauchon's chagrin, the chief notary of the trial, Guillaume Manchon, who had been in charge of recording every question and answer, refused to attend. He had been deeply moved by the execution of Jeanne – he testified later that he had been unable to find any peace for long after – and he now informed Cauchon that as the trial was over, he had no further official funcion, and anything he might say could have no legal value; this, in effect, was a subtle professional *caveat* that anything Cauchon and his lackeys might add to the record now would also be worthless as evidence.

While the military campaign was getting under way, the English also began a campaign of propaganda based on the trial and execution of Jeanne. A week after her death, a letter signed by the boy king Henry VI was sent to all the kings and dukes of Christian Europe. It consisted of a summary of her career and death, of how she had been deceived into various errors against the faith, had repented at her trial and confessed that her voices were evil, but had relapsed into heresy through pride. Other letters from the king to Cauchon and some other bishops assured them that 'if any person who was engaged in this trial should be sued on account of the trial or its consquences, we shall aid and defend them in any legal action at our own cost and expense.' In a letter a few weeks later, the king urged all the bishops, dukes, nobles, and public officials in all the cities of France, to make known the truth about Jeanne la Pucelle, by preaching and other means, and especially that she had herself admitted that her so-called heavenly voices had been evil and had led her into heresy, for which she had suffered just punishment. Joining in the campaign of vilification, the theological professors at the University of Paris wrote to the Pope and the College of Cardinals giving their own defamatory version of the life and career of the heretical Jeanne la Pucelle.

Whatever comfort he may have derived from the royal guarantee of financial indemnification, Cauchon was to be disappointed in his hope of ecclesiastical advancement because of his services to Bedford and Cardinal Beaufort. Instead of the position he coveted, Archbishop of Reims, he was appointed Bishop of Liseux six months after the death of Jeanne. However, his career as a diplomat continued to flourish. He was present at the coronation of King Henry VI in Paris on 16 December 1431, and he was employed as an emissary of the king on many important missions, even at general councils of the church. Later, he visited England several times in connection with the peace negotiations between the two countries, and also the liberation of the Duke of Orléans after twenty-five years as a prisoner in England. In between all his public functions and journeys, Cauchon must have wondered in quiet moments what future generations would make of the story of the young woman whose death he had engineered to further his own ambitions and those of his English masters. He would have had some food for thought when, only four years after her death, a mystery play was staged in Orléans telling the story of the siege and its heroine, Jeanne la Pucelle. All the resources of the city were put to use, and the citizens set up stages at every gate of the city. The manuscript of that first play is extant. It would be followed by many more in every century, and by many films as soon as that medium of entertainment became available. Cauchon did not live to see Charles VII commence, however belatedly in 1450, the process that would reverse the verdict of the 1431 trial. He died suddenly, while being shaved by his barber, at his episcopal residence in Rouen, on 18 December 1442, and was buried with pomp and ceremony in his episcopal church at Lisieux.

The military campaign that had started promisingly for the English soon began to falter. A year after the execution of Jeanne, the Duchess of Bedford died. She was the sister of the Duke of Burgundy and a strong influence in the alliance between him and the English. However, that alliance was always based on the Duke of Burgundy's own political ambitions – some historians even suggesting that he might have seen himself as eventually becoming King of France, or of establishing a kingdom of his own comprising Lorraine in the east of France and his territories to the north in the Low Countries. When the Duke of Bedford remarried within six months of the death of his wife, the Duke of Burgundy was displeased on personal and political grounds. Bedford's new bride was the seventeen-year-old daughter of a vassal of Burgundy, thus giving Bedford and the English a potential area of influence in the Duke's own domains. He began to consider making peace with his cousin, Charles VII – as the French chronicler comments, he had always been French in his blood. English delegates were invited to tripartite peace talks at Arras in August 1435, but they soon left, perhaps on realising the drift of Burgundy's intentions.

The Duke of Bedford himself died at Rouen a month later, in the castle where Jeanne la Pucelle had been a prisoner for five months. When that news reached the peace conference at Arras, it hastened the treaty between Charles VII and the Duke of Burgundy that ended the civil war between the French and made the position of the English in Franch more insecure. A year later, in 1436, the French took Paris, and Jeanne's prediction that the English would suffer great losses was fulfilled. Another of her predictions, that the Duke of Orléans would return from England, came to pass in 1440.

During his twenty-five years in comfortable captivity in

England, Duke Charles of Orléans had been kept well informed of events in France – he had even been able, according to the chivalric customs of his class, to conduct the business of his territory through delegates – and he now showed his appreciation of what Jeanne la Pucelle had done for his city and his people. Jeanne's mother, Isabelle Romée, was now widowed, and her eldest son also having died she was in poor circumstances in spite of the family having been ennobled by Charles VII. Jeanne's brother, Pierre, who served at her side all through her campaigns and was taken prisoner with her at Compiègne, had been held for ransom, eventually gaining his freedom only by selling his wife's inheritance. Along with his mother, his wife and son, Pierre was now invited by the council of Orléans to come and live there. Isabelle was given a house and a pension, while the Duke himself later made over an island in the Loire to Pierre and his family.

A year before this, the people of Orléans had gone through a different experience when a woman arrived in the city claiming to be Jeanne. There were many people in France who would willingly believe that God had intervened to save Jeanne in some way, or that she was now returning from heaven to complete her mission of driving the English out of France. Even the youngest of Jeanne's three brothers seems to have accepted the impostor for a while, although there is some suspicion that he may have been hoping to profit by her impersonation. There were several other attempts at resurrecting Jeanne, but they all faded out quickly.

Although the young King Henry VI made a new effort to reverse the tide of French victory – Charles VII had re-taken Normandy, entering its capital, Rouen, on 10 November 1449 – the army for which he had even pawned the crown jewels had no success, suffering a heavy defeat at Formigny in April 1450. Meanwhile, Charles VII, at Rouen, was obviously reminded of what had happened in the old marketplace of that city on 30 May 1431, and of all that the young woman named Jeanne la Pucelle had done for him. He would have been shown the true records of her trial by the notary, Guillaume Manchon, and there were many people, both laymen and theologians like the Dominican friars at the church of Saint-Jacques, who had now, for many years, been discussing the pros and cons of what would come to be regarded as one of the most notoriously unjust trials in history. Whether King Charles ever suffered any pangs of conscience in the years since he had abandoned Jeanne to her fate is as much a secret as the one she confided to him at their first meeting, by which he was convinced to accept her heaven-sent aid in his cause. It must also have been obvious to Charles that Jeanne was already being regarded all over France as a heroine and a martyr, and that his failure to ransom or rescue her from the English was likely to become a lasting blot on his own reputation. A reversal of the verdict of the 1431 trial, besides clearing the name of Jeanne, would help to erase or at least dilute that blot.

At Rouen, on 15 February 1450, Charles dictated the letter that set in motion the process of rehabilitation of Jeanne la Pucelle. He ordered his counsellor, Guillaume Bouillé, to set up a commission that would investigate everything connected with the previous trial, to collect evidence and information from all possible sources, and present it to the king and his council. The first person to be interviewed was the notary of the trial, Guillaume Manchon, followed by the friars at Saint-Jacques and the usher, Jean Massieu, who had been in charge of Jeanne from the first day of her imprisonment to the day of her execution. The result of this preliminary inquiry quickly established beyond any doubt that Jeanne, although a prisoner of war and therefore a political prisoner, had been put on trial for heresy in a church court and sentenced there. This raised a new problem – the verdict of a church court in a trial for heresy could only be overturned by a similar court. As if guided by Jeanne herself or by her heavenly voices in order to set up such a court, Pope Nicholas V, whose proclamation of the Jubilee year in 1450 drew thousands of pilgrims to Rome from all over Europe, sent as his legate to France a relative of the king himself, Guillaume d'Estouteville. This noble ecclesiastic was well aware of the history of Jeanne and of the king's initiative in the cause of her rehabilitation. He could not have wished for a more enthusiastic supporter than the new Inquisitor of France, Jean Bréhal, who was actually prior of the Dominican convent of Saint-Jacques in Rouen.

With the aid of two Italian prelates who were members of the legate's own staff and experts in church law, the Legate and the Inquisitor studied the original transcript of the trial provided by the notary, Guillaume Manchon. A series of twelve articles was then drawn up, corresponding to the twelve articles used by Cauchon and his aides, to serve as a formula of interrogation; but when these were put to the first key witnesses, including the notary himself, who had already been questioned by the king's counsellor, it was found that they needed to be expanded into twenty-seven articles in order to cover every aspect of the illegality of the first trial. Every witness would be asked to confirm or deny the truth of each article.

Some of the witnesses interviewed were persons who had served as judges or assesssors in the first trial, and some of the articles, adverting to the threats and pressure applied to them by the English, incidentally cleared them of personal culpability. Some such who might not have been thus indemnified, including Bishop Pierre Cauchon himself, were dead. Nicholas Midy, the preacher who harangued Jeanne in a sermon on the morning of her execution, had died of leprosy, and the foul-tongued cleric, Jean d'Estivet, who insulted her in her cell and also inserted obscene innuendoes in the expanded report of her trial, was found dead in a sewer seven years after her death.

At the end of this investigation, the Inquisitor of France, Jean Bréhal, made a digest of the evidence, called a *summarium*, which had to be submitted to church lawyers and theologians for their judgement – Cauchon had been obliged to do likewise, although, as has been seen, the text of what he sent out to the experts was very different from what was to be found in the original transcript of Jeanne's trial. All of this was only the gathering of sufficient evidence to put before the Pope, the only person who could authorise a new trial in the case of a condemned heretic. Jean

Bréhal went to Rome with his evidence, and the new Pope, Calixtus III, duly gave the necessary permission for the nullification trial, in which the family of Jeanne herself would be the plaintiffs, with three bishops acting as the Pope's own observers in the case. In November 1455, these three prelates officiated at the formal inauguration of the process in Notre Dame in Paris. The first person asked to make a statement regarding Jeanne la Pucelle was her own mother, Isabelle Romée. Accompanied by a group of people from Orléans who had come to support the old woman, she came forward and placed on record a brief summary of the life and death of her daughter.

From Paris the inquest moved to Rouen, where witnesses were heard in the archbishop's palace. In all, 115 witnesses were interrogated. The judges then sent a delegation of inquiry to Domrémy, where the inhabitants were once more questioned about Jeanne's childhood and youth – as with the other inquiries, there was nothing sensational, and nothing negative, to report; the most common memory of those who had known Jeanne was that she was just like everybody else. The final inquest was held at Orléans, where testimony was taken from people of all classes, common citizens offering their recollections alongside those of dukes and military commanders who had fought in Jeanne's campaigns. On 7 July 1456, the verdict was proclaimed in the palace of the Archbishop of Rouen: the first trial of Jeanne was declared to be null and void. Official ceremonies and celebrations greeted the verdict all over France. In Orléans, a festival in memory of Jeanne la Pucelle was held, with Jeanne's aged mother as the guest of honour. She died two years later.

Although it was apparent, *inter alia*, as the interrogations and inquiries proceeded, that Jeanne, from her first appearance on the public scene to the moment of her death at the stake, was a very holy woman, the idea that she might be officially recognised as such by the church was overshadowed for a long time by her idealisation as a political prisoner and the iconic heroine of France. It was left to Felix Dupanloup, Bishop of Orléans from 1849 to 1878, to call universal attention to the personal sanctity of Jeanne d'Arc, as she had now become known. He got the bishops of France interested in the case to the extent that, in 1869, they sent a petition to Pope Pius IX asking permission to begin yet another investigation into the life and death of Jeanne. The process continued under subsequent bishops until finally, in 1909, Pope Pius X beatified Jeanne. The First World War intervened in this as in many other matters – in that war, the warrior girl of Orléans was invoked as a patron of France by the soldiers trudging towards the trenches – until at last, on 6 May 1920, the name of Jeanne d'Arc was prefixed by the word *Sainte* as she was added to the roll of those whom the Catholic Church officially acknowledges as persons who, having lived lives of heroic virtue on this earth, are now enjoying the promised reward of eternal happiness with God in heaven.

Long before this ultimate official recognition of her personal sanctity, Jeanne d'Arc had been acclaimed by *vox populi* as a heroine and a saint. Books and plays had spread her fame in many languages, and the new mass medium of film was soon added. Cities and towns in France erected statues in her honour, the most notable being the equestrian statue of the warrior La Pucelle before the cathedral at Reims and the contrasting image of her death at the stake which stands outside the Sainte Jeanne d'Arc church in the Old Market Square at Rouen. A splendid equestrian statue in the Riverside Park in New York, unveiled by the French Ambassador in 1915, was a portent, perhaps, of the imminent involvement of the United States in the horrors of the Great War in which France had already lost so many thousands of its own soldiers. A statue of special significance is the one to be seen in Winchester Cathedral. Opposite the tomb of Cardinal Henry Beaufort, the political churchman who instigated and presided over her trial, the statue of Jeanne in shining armour, with her sword held upright in her right hand, was erected in 1923, three years after her canonisation, by the Anglican diocese of Winchester, as a mark of reparation to Jeanne La Pucelle.